A COMMONPLACE BOOK ON TEACHING AND LEARNING

Reflections on learning processes, teaching methods, and their effects on scientific literacy

PASCAL DE CAPRARIIS

authorHOUSE®

AuthorHouse™
1663 Liberty Drive
Bloomington, IN 47403
www.authorhouse.com
Phone: 1-800-839-8640

First published by AuthorHouse   9/28/2010

ISBN: 978-1-4520-5371-4 (sc)
ISBN: 978-1-4520-5372-1 (e)

Printed in the United States of America
Bloomington, Indiana

This book is printed on acid-free paper.

For Nancy

"Age cannot wither her, nor custom stale her infinite variety."
Shakespeare

CONTENTS

PREFACE

Caveat Lector: The reader should be aware that although this book is about teaching and learning, nothing in it is based on rigorous research in educational psychology. Instead, everything that follows consists of my personal opinions, ones that are based on my experiences teaching, and on my reading and cogitating.

The format of the book is a little unusual because I decided to use the structure of a commonplace book, in which commonplace items that one comes across in one's life are jotted down for future reference in a journal. In some cases, *e.g.* in the book by Charles Curtis (see the references) each item serves as a quotation that is followed by elaboration. Other examples of this genre (*e.g.* the one by W.H. Auden) forgo most if not all of the elaboration, in which case, the entries in the book give some insight into the kinds of things that interested the compiler, but do not indicate how he thought about them.

My addition to this genre is closer to that of Curtis than to Auden's. The idea here is to let the quotations set up discussions about topics of interest to me. My intent was to end up with a loosely coupled but reasonably coherent set of ideas within each chapter.

This goal was pursued by seeing to it that a substantial number of quotations within a chapter are at least somewhat related. But as you will see, sometimes one "elaboration" triggers another, so not every commentary in this book is directly tied to a quotation.

One advantage of this format is that the reader can open the book nearly anywhere and find an idea that can be considered independently of other parts of the book. The intent is to provide on every page stepping stones that allow the reader to go a bit further by mulling over an idea. To assist the reader who opens the book randomly, the discussions are broken up into paragraphs that are shorter than normal (as they are on this page). In addition, three-line gaps separate paragraphs that can be considered independently of the previous ones.

The book was compiled from a journal I kept for about 25 years as I taught, first in a high school while writing my dissertation, and then at a university. Over the years I jotted down in spiral-bound notebooks anything interesting I heard on the radio, or read in the newspapers or books, thoughts about things to do in my classes, etc. That is, I recorded many years worth of "commonplaces." Some of the items were one or two lines long, others were extensive notes taken from some source. The entries were entered irregularly; several might be entered one evening and then weeks might pass before the next one went in.

Even after I began using a personal computer extensively, I continued to include material in the notebooks because it is easier to jot something down on paper while reading a book than to put the book down to type something into a word processing file. By the time I shifted entirely to the computer I had eight fairly thick notebooks to mine for the material in this book. Even though much of what was in those volumes did not pertain to teaching or education in general, and even though I did not use everything in them that *did* pertain to education, I found enough material to structure the discussions on the four topics covered in this book.

I suspect that the average reader will conclude that I am a very gloomy guy because of the negative comments in some of the discussions in the book. In my defense, I will note that most of the negativity is directed at the impersonal classroom atmosphere caused by an increase in class size over the last few decades, and at the belief that the use of various technologies can overcome that effect. I taught large-enrollment introductory science classes for many years and became discouraged with the results because putting large numbers of people in a large classroom is an efficient way to teach a course but is not the way to get students to learn much about the subject. In addition, these courses are not the way to convince students that science is the exciting enterprise that I have always found it to be. If I seem gloomy, so be it.

Now something about opinions. There is a distressing attitude in today's society that beliefs need not be supported by evidence or logic; that one person's opinion is just as valid as anyone else's; that education and experience carry no more weight than the ideas someone heard in a bar one night. I reject that attitude because if everything is of equal value, nothing is important. I am sure that no one will be entranced by each and every idea presented here, so some of what follows will be accepted by readers and some will be rejected. That is fine, because rejection requires as much analysis as acceptance, and analysis is the key to progress.

Because everything in this book represents my personal opinions, nothing is sacrosanct. If I stick my chin out by saying something another person feels is not reasonable, I will not be surprised to get a gentle (or perhaps, not so gentle) reminder that I am not infallible. Comments are welcome. They can be sent to decaprariis@sbcglobal.net

TEACHING AND LEARNING

"Walker, there is no pathway
You make the pathway while you walk"
Antonio Machado

These lines provide a good introduction to a discussion of teaching Because they say clearly what instructors have to recognize - that there is no correct way to learn how to teach. As you work at your profession, you will learn how to work at your profession, and your path will differ from mine, because you and I are different people with different experiences. But there are some basic principles, so let's start by discussing the important distinction between teaching and learning.

A number of years ago I had several discussions with the chairman of my department about evaluating candidates for teaching positions. In the interview process the faculty tried to determine which of them would be likely to do a good job in the classroom, and once they were hired, we tried to determine how good a job they were doing. The chairman felt that it was not possible to specify all of the things a good teacher does in the classroom. There are too many variables to assume such a list would be inclusive, so he was not sure that a list of things that teachers *should* do in the classroom would be useful. Instead, he felt that it was much easier to make a list of things that teachers *should not* do. If we could make new teachers aware of the items on such a list, the transition from graduate school to a teaching position should be smoother.

The implication is that if I am *not* doing the things on the second list, whatever I *am* doing in the classroom must be acceptable. That is, if I am not clearly a bad teacher, I am either a good teacher, or I can become one. That logic is not really sound because, as with the first list, we cannot be sure that we know everything one should not do.

But that is quibbling. Making sure that someone is not doing a number of things that contribute to bad teaching would be a major accomplishment, and depending on the length of the list of things one should not do, it should be possible to improve the teaching styles of many beginners.

On the other hand, that goal is insufficient because it concentrates on what the *teacher* is doing and makes no reference to what the *students* are doing. Regardless of what I do in the classroom and how well I do it, the ultimate test of teaching is to answer the question: "what are the students learning and how well are they learning it?"

> "A university is "Mark Hopkins on one end of a log and a student on the other."
> **President James Garfield**

Ideally, a class should be something like a conversation: Socrates talking to an acquaintance, Mark Hopkins, to a student. Talking to students results in learning most effectively when it involves two-way conversations, and that model of learning is best suited to very small groups. When anything but very small groups is involved, mere "presentation" may not be effective.

Of course, traditionally, one-way communications *have* been effective in teaching. Consider how cultural material has always been communicated. The presentation usually starts with something like:

> "Sing, Goddess, of the wrath of Peleus' son Achilles..."

or

> "Coyote was going there."

Unlike conversations that require back and forth interactions, stories merely require that the audience have some familiarity with the material. In the first example, the storyteller is telling the audience that his tale about the war with Troy is being mediated by his muse, a goddess, so what they are about to hear is due to her, not to him. In such a case the audience knows that the story will be important, as well as entertaining. The second example, from the Hopi tradition, involves an elder starting a tale that has moral implications for the young members of the tribe. Each example starts by introducing the context of the story: a divinely inspired tale or an important moral lesson. In each case the audience is familiar enough with the context that the teller of the tale can continue fruitfully.

Now consider a typical classroom environment today and ask yourself if the audience will be as rapt as those who are listening to a storyteller. Then consider the reasons for the difference between the traditional and the academic ways of teaching. Even when cultural information is being transmitted today (say a class on the U.S. Constitution), the emphasis is on facts to be learned, not on moral lessons. Students tend to be more concerned with passing the next test than on internalizing the material for a lifetime.

Of course, reasons exist for the difference. A gifted storyteller could construct a tale about the American Revolution, the period following it, and the development of the Constitution, but how many instructors could present such a tale to a group of students as the epic poets did? I cannot picture myself strumming a lyre, while telling about George Washington, "the father of our country" in dactylic hexameters as Homer spoke of the death of Hector, "tamer of horses." And even if I could, how would students demonstrate mastery of the lessons in such a tale?

So how is mastery usually demonstrated?

Evaluating students' knowledge in traditionally-taught courses, especially large-enrollment courses, usually involves multiple-choice tests because instructors do not have the time to grade several hundred essay questions each semester. Unfortunately, most college instructors are not trained in the design of multiple-choice questions, so the assumption that the test results are diagnostic of student learning is suspect. But no matter how well these tests are designed, they cannot provide as accurate a measure of a student's mastery of a subject as is often claimed. The reason is that the tests pertain to what was said in class or written in the textbook, not to what the students perceived about the material. The difference between presentation and perception is recognized by most teachers but rarely do we have a way to bridge the gap between them. So we usually do not really know what the students know about a subject, just how well they recorded what we said in class.

Even if we assume that students' scores on a standardized test are a good indication of their understanding of the material being tested, the scores just indicate their understanding today. But what will they understand tomorrow? And how can we know that? To answer those questions, imagine that you give a multiple-choice test to a class, and then at the next class meeting, without having announced your intent to do so, give the same test to the same students. The average grade of the class will probably be the same but the grades of individual students will vary. Some of the students will receive approximately the same grade the second time, but some will do better and others will do worse.

A few students will do better the second time because they looked over the material after the previous test. Others will do better because they just happened to have a better day. Some students will do worse the second time because they had put the material completely out of their minds and are outraged at being forced to take the test again. Others will do worse because they may have to take a test for another course that day and are feeling the stress brought on by your surprise. The point is that many aspects of the students' mental states will have changed between the two class meetings, so we should not be surprised if large variations in individual grades occur. How can we say which grade, if either, represents a particular student's knowledge?

Taking this idea a step further, consider the following *gedanken* experiment. Assume it is possible to give the same test to the same students for 10 classes in a row, without them realizing what you are doing. In all likelihood, each student would get six to eight different scores, and for some students, the range of the scores could be quite large, depending on personal and emotional conditions over which we have no control (e.g. illness, an automobile accident, a bad relationship, etc.). During that time period every student's ability to respond to test questions will have been passed through a variety of filters, each of which tends to affect their ability to read the questions carefully. That will lead to variations in individual scores, even if the average class grades on the 10 sets of tests were the same. With several different independent scores, which of them would be the correct measure of a student's "mastery?"

We cannot do this kind of experiment of course, but the idea illustrates the point that when measured with standardized tests, mastery appears to be a fuzzy concept, regardless of how well the tests are constructed.

To elaborate on the idea of someone "having a better day," I work on the crossword puzzles in the *New York Times* six days a week (I do not get the Sunday edition). The puzzle on Thursday is usually quite difficult, so sometimes I get no more than about one half completed. On those occasions, if I put it down and wait until the next day, quite often I can fill in more, sometimes a lot more, of the puzzle (I am *very* pleased when I finish it). Am I smarter the second day? No, the extra time just seems to allow me to circumvent mental barriers that prevented me from understanding some clues the first day. The same degree of success with the puzzles in the Friday and Saturday editions does not occur very often, even when my attempts are spread out over several days because the clues seem to be an order of magnitude more obscure than those on Thursday.

Crossword puzzles are not vocabulary tests: they are tests of how well one can associate one idea with another. That is the basis of all true testing, and for that reason the word "association" will appear throughout this book.

In contrast to the variations in each individual student's performance, is the stability of the average grade on a test. The particular mix of students in a course each semester is random and, since we have no control over who takes the course, we should expect random variations in performance. In fact, fluctuations should be considered to be a natural characteristic of the system. Normally there will be several (many?) causes of variations in students' scores on tests. If there is no reason to think that any one of the causes is more important than any other, the Central Limit Theorem suggests that the "average" response to the test questions will be reasonably stable from semester to semester. That is, the average grades on standardized tests should not vary significantly. That is what I observed semester after semester teaching introductory geology courses at a university. The average grades on the tests I gave ranged between 70 and 76.

Unfortunately, it is easy to decide that a test is a valid measure of students' achievements if the average grade remains about the same from semester to semester. But when we rely on a stable measure of performance, such as the average grade, we tend to neglect the variance of the grade distribution. We tend to neglect the variance (however large) because we assume that some students are bound to do well and others to do poorly, as long as we are dealing with what appears to be a Normal Distribution.

> Isn't it interesting how the word "Normal" affects our perception of the matter?

One wonders if the students really matter, or if only the behavior of the class matters. It is not realistic to eliminate standardized tests, but the sole use of them to evaluate students does not seem fair to the students.

Our lectures are given to students but the tests we give them measure the performance of the group more accurately than that of any given student. Confusing the members of a class or assemblage of things with the class itself is the kind of logical fallacy that Bertrand Russell's theory of Logical Types was devised to confront (Unlike Russell himself, Gregory Bateson discussed this concept clearly). A commonly used explanation of this fallacy invokes the fact that the class of elephants is not an elephant; it has neither a trunk nor large ears, so statements that can be made about an individual elephant cannot be carried over to the class, and vice versa.

In the present context, the assemblage of students is not a student. The assemblage is not an entity in the same sense that a person is. The assemblage cannot learn the material, regardless of the grade "it" receives on a test (the average grade). Only students can learn. So what can we do to determine how much they learn? Characterizing students based on the difference between their grades and the average grade of the assemblage of students says nothing about what the students know about the subject. Regardless of the average grade, if a student's grade on a multiple-choice test is 70%, does that really mean that the student *understands* 70% of the material covered in the test? What percentage of correct answers is due to reading ability? What percentage of it is due to luck (either good or bad luck) on the day of the test? These are questions that cannot be answered by finding new ways to present content. We need to know what is happening at the other end of the communications channel.

I knew an instructor once who put a great deal of effort into writing multiple-choice questions. He felt that the questions on his tests were valid indicators of students' understanding of the material because he made sure that all five choices for each question seemed plausible. That is, one choice *was* correct but the other four *seemed* correct on first reading. He felt that students who answered a question correctly must understand the material because they had to eliminate the four other choices that seemed at first to be correct.

That is an interesting argument, but it ignores an important point. It may be that students who get a particular question correct understand the material in that question but it does not follow that students who do not answer that question correctly do not understand the material. The reason is that reading skills play a large part in the ability to answer multiple-choice questions correctly, and in principle, the tests are supposed to be related to content, not to reading skills. I can think of no way to distinguish between reading skills and knowledge of content on his tests, so, considering the pressure on students to finish the test in a specified period of time, the gentleman may well have been testing reading skills rather than understanding.

"Some students find it easier to deal with failure than with limited success."
Julius Getman

An interesting statement. If I do just enough to get a D in a class, I may realize that with a little more work I could have had a C, and even perhaps, a B. That realization puts the blame for barely succeeding entirely on me. It is my fault that I did not do better. But if I get an F in the class, I can rationalize failure by saying the course was too hard for me; that no matter how hard I might have worked, I would not have received a passing grade, so it is not really my fault that I failed the course.

This is a problem that cannot be solved by any amount of effort on the part of a teacher to do a better job in the classroom, because it represents a cultural conflict.

On the one hand, society expects students to attend school and expects the schools to prepare the students for their futures. On the other hand, the academic environment is sufficiently distinct from the "real lives" of the students that some (many?) of them do not recognize the importance of succeeding in school, so they are open to ways to rationalize failure.

That's "... the news from Lake Wobegon, where all of
the women are strong, all the men are good looking,
and all of the children are above average."
Garrison Keillor

I guess that those who wrote the "No Child Left Behind" legislation do not listen to National Public Radio. They did not seem to realize that in the real world of the classroom and the multiple choice tests students take there, not everyone can be above average.

Establishing an arbitrary minimum score and requiring that every student in a school exceed that score is equivalent to requiring that everyone be above average.

Another problem that students face is the lack of coherence in many (most?) university curricula. Imagine someone who goes into a new country every 50 minutes. The natives of the countries are the teachers students deal with, each of whom speaks a different language. Richard Lanham used this metaphor effectively by saying:

"In this ethnographic map of the university, life is
much easier for us than for the students. We stay
in our own country. We know it is the best country,
indeed the inevitable country for anyone of intelligence
and taste, - else why would we have chosen to dwell
there? We also know that in other department-
countries the inhabitants speak a barbarous jargon.
But is that not normal? They are, after all barbarians.
What else would you expect them to speak? We
ourselves speak the natural language of God, and it is

> our sacred obligation to teach that language to students
> who pass our way."

Is there any wonder that students are frustrated by the courses they take? Learning something new is hard enough without having to do the equivalent of jumping through hoops of different sizes in different disciplines.

The quality control expert W. Edwards Deming once said that a hotel is built and organized for the convenience of management.

Even if we assume that all of the teachers are good at what they do, it is clear that we cannot guarantee that students are learning what the instructors think they are supposed to learn. Perhaps we should concentrate less on how an instructor is teaching, and more on what the students are learning.

So what does it mean to "learn" something?

One approach to defining learning is to say that it involves associating the content provided in what one hears with what one already knows. The concept "association" is important. Roger Schank feels that the learning process is analogous to assigning a label to an entry in a database.

In principle, the person who can assign a variety of labels to the content provided in a course will be able to call upon the material later in a variety of contexts. That person will recognize the relevance of what is already known to what is being provided today. So an instructor must provide content *and* provide ways to label that content so it can be recalled later. Two jobs, not one. Doing just the first is easy, but doing *just* the first results in students capable of doing nothing more than rote learning of their poorly organized lecture notes as they study for tests.

But how are labels assigned to material?

Contexts are important because they provide ways to assign labels. Consider the students in an introductory course in Oceanography. Those who took a course in Chemistry the year before will recognize associations between the material on the properties of seawater and some of the material they learned previously in Chemistry. Labels are assigned to this year's material based on what was learned in the past. Students will not remember everything (or even most of) what they learned about the water molecule in the past, but a context will exist that allows labeling of the new material. In effect, the old material is analogous to a peg on the wall on which you can hang the hat you bought today. Tomorrow, you can easily find the hat when you leave the house.

But analogies can only do so much. The hat does not affect the peg, whereas in the educational context, the labels are bi-directional, in that knowledge of last year's material is modified by the new material. New material is overlaid onto old material, resulting in what Schank calls "semantic memory."

Semantic memory is an excellent description because it associates the material with meaning.

Old information about water chemistry is not replaced by what one learns about the properties of seawater: it is added to. A semester or two later, if students must deal with the properties of water they will not think "In one course I learned this about water and in another I learned that." Instead, when they recall something about water they will recall aspects of the whole. The phase relationships between our learning experiences are lost because the time sequence of the learning is not important. This is a useful way to construct memories. We learn from experience by broadening the spectrum of what kinds of things can happen, not by keeping track of everything that has happened and the order in which they happened.

Back to the crossword puzzles. The easy puzzles involve only recall; someone with a reasonable working vocabulary can call up definitions and finish them. But the challenging puzzles require complicated associations, not recall. I did one once in which the clue for a seven letter answer was the phrase "bad setting." After rejecting answers that involved machinery, I concentrated on the word "bad." Eventually I realized that if I pronounced it as "bod" it would be the word for spa in German (e.g. such as the one at Marienbad). And in fact, the answer turned out to be "Germany." I have no idea how I realized that I should consider a foreign word, but getting to that realization clearly required that I have a variety of labels assigned to the word bad.

Schank claims that the overlay process results in memories that are hierarchically structured. He notes that most people will agree that flounders have fins because they know that fish have fins (even if they are not sure of the purpose of fins) and that a flounder is a fish (even if they have never seen a flounder). This organization is useful because it allows us to relate to things around us more efficiently. The fine details of a subject rarely are so important that I cannot carry on a conversation about it without knowing them. Knowing that something called a flounder exists may be sufficient for me to take part in a conversation about ocean resources.

If memories are hierarchically structured, delivering a lecture in outline form should be an efficient way to present information because the relationships between levels in the outline should be the key that students need to organize what they write in their notes (and store in their memories). It is true that the outline structure commonly used in the delivery of lectures displays relationships between aspects of the content without the need to specifically mention them, but regardless of the attractiveness of Schank's argument, only academics think consciously in outline form, so one might well wonder how effective that technique really is in a lecture. After all, courses are taken by students, not by teachers. Even when I projected an outline of my lectures onto a screen, it did not always end up in students' notes in a recognizable way. Or, even when it was copied down correctly, not too many students recognized the need to fill in between sections of the outline, using what I was saying during the lecture.

The real problem with using an outline as the structure of a lecture is that the students are not concerned with relationships or labels. Instead, they are trying to record what they hear sufficiently accurately that it will make sense to them a few weeks later, when they study for a test. And many of them think that they have to write down as much of what you say as is possible. Regardless of how their memories might work, most students are not used to organizing material in outline form because most conversations (even between professors) consist of serial sequences of thoughts, not structured presentations.

William Hazlitt gave an example of an exception to the statement about structured conversations. In an essay on walking, he said:

> "My old friend Coleridge...could go on in the most
> delightful explanatory way over hill and dale a
> summer's day, and convert a landscape into a didactic
> poem or a Pindaric ode. 'He talked far above singing.'"

Few of us have those skills, so regardless of the structure of a class presentation, most students hear sequences of thoughts that they try to record in real time. That is an extraordinarily difficult task.

> "People who are able to construct an intellectual
> framework assume that students should be able to
> also."
> **Julius Getman**

Just how difficult is it to take a decent set of lecture notes? Academics tend to assume that students - at least the better ones - will approach learning the way academics do. But the hierarchically structured lecture is not similar in any way to the manner in which people learn things outside of school.

After I had been giving lectures to large classes for more than 15 years I thought I was doing a good job, so I wondered why my students often had trouble taking a good set of notes. I decided to find out by performing an experiment on myself. Lectures in the introductory Psychology course at my university had been put on videotape and were made available to students in the class at the library, so I decided to watch some of the tapes, as beginning students did. I had never taken a course in the subject, so with regard to the content at least, I assumed that I was as much a beginner as the average Freshman taking the class.

Over a period of four days I checked out the tapes for four lectures and watched them on a monitor in a learning laboratory. I took notes in a notebook as if I had been in a regular lecture, in that I went through each tape only once, and did not replay parts that I did not understand during the "lecture." Then I typed up my notes and stored them in computer files so I could examine them later.

Three of the four lectures were delivered by the same instructor, and as a check on teaching styles, the fourth lecture I chose was given by a different fellow. They were all "talking head" lectures, in that no illustrations were used. The presentations were remarkably well-done, in that the instructors always faced the camera and presented the material as smoothly as the anchors on the evening news programs.

The experience was educational. I had no difficulty in taking notes in the first two lectures; it was clear to me that the instructor was delivering the material in outline form, so I found it easy to take notes in that format (Of course, I do not know how many students in the class recognized that the material was organized that way). The outline form preserved relationships between the categories that the instructor felt were important. I felt that if I had to take a test on the material in a few weeks my notes allow me to do well on the test. The third lecture was less structured, so I had to force my notes to fit into the outline form, and the fourth lecture, by the other instructor, seemed to have no structure at all. The outline form I tried to impose on that set of notes was not consistent; it was clearly a Procrustean fit to the material. My notes were little more than a string of comments about the several topics covered in the lecture. That bothered me because if I, a professional student, could not take a good set of notes from the lecture, how could beginning students do it?

So I talked about my experiment with the chairman of the Psychology department, who had supervised the taping of the lectures. He was not surprised by the results, saying that the topics covered in the fourth lecture were not organized well because the profession was not in agreement about how to do it. So the instructor had no choice but to present little more than a list of topics. The instructor went through the list of all of the ideas that the profession felt could explain the phenomena, without noting that the profession was not sure about how to organize the material. Studying from my notes for a test on that topic would have involved memorizing a great deal of apparently unrelated material.

To be fair, students in the Psychology course were not totally dependent on the lectures I viewed. They had a textbook, small group sessions, and laboratory sessions. So an unstructured lecture was not a disaster; in fact, to a perceptive student, it could provide a source of questions to be asked at the small group sessions. But I wonder how many students taking an introductory course in a discipline realize that a certain vagueness in a lecture is not necessarily their fault, but that it may be inherent in the material.

I concluded from the experiment that students who are aware of the utility of the outline form can often take a decent set of notes. But they may well be frustrated when the lecture is not structured.

When what is presented is not structured we cannot expect *any* students to end up with a coherent set of notes. When the delivery seems to be no more than a "stream of consciousness" presentation students cannot be expected to get much out of the lecture.

> Teaching is going on in such cases, but not much learning.

I seem to be contradicting myself here. First I said that students do not recognize the utility of the outline form and then I said that if lectures are not in outline form students will not be able to take a good set of notes. There is a simple way to address this contradiction, namely to note the impersonal nature of the large-lecture format. The problem is the format, not how the material is presented. One cannot interact with hundreds of students, and without interaction, little learning is occurring. Some instructors can overcome the impersonal atmosphere that is present in large classes better than others, but it is not realistic to expect everyone to do the kind of job the most charismatic instructors do, and one wonders if even they can be sufficiently charismatic in every single lecture. Someone once said that only the mediocre can be at their best every day.

> "Medea should refrain from murdering her children on the stage."
> **Horace, *Instructions***

That is good advice. The imaginations of the members of the audience will construct a much more vivid picture of what is happening backstage as smoke billows out through the scenery and as the screams of Medea and her children are heard, than anything the playwright can show onstage. In an analogous manner, if you want students to develop an understanding of a subject, you should let them infer things about it.

> Students should be allowed to construct personalized mental images, instead of merely being told how to think about the matter.

There is no point in telling students how they should learn. You have to let them discover for themselves what is needed. This pertains to the problem of determining how to assign labels. Every instructor will approach the task differently, but at the risk of being too specific, here is an example of how I would recommend doing it.

I taught about earthquakes in several courses, so I will use as an example, the New Madrid earthquakes of 1811-1812. Although earthquakes can occur anywhere, the existing paradigm holds that the large ones are supposed to occur only along tectonic plate boundaries, such as the San Andreas fault zone in California. But the three very large events that occurred near New Madrid, Missouri between December 1811 and February, 1812 occurred in the middle of a plate. Because they were unusual, and because I taught in the Mid-West, I usually devoted at least one class to them in my introductory Geology courses. So here is one way to structure the learning (*not* the teaching) process.

I think of earthquakes in terms of:

> 1) the magnitudes of the events - very large
> 2) their location - in the middle of a plate - very rare

3) their recurrence interval - very long, as far as we can tell.

These three aspects are not independent because (3) follows from (2), but they are important aspects. If I tell students that this is the way I think about the subject they will write it down in their notes and memorize the aspects when studying for the next test. But they will not "own" those labels because they did not create them. The task is to create an exercise that will let them develop their own labels, even if the ones they develop are not quite the ones I use.

For example, one could:

> Give them data about magnitudes, locations and frequencies of earthquakes in California and in the Mid-West.

> Then tell them to separate "signal from noise." That is, have them group the data in different ways, and let them determine the groupings.

> Then have them tell a "story" about it. That is, have them write a paragraph or two summarizing their results.

If they can write a narrative in which the frequency of the events clearly distinguishes those in the center of a plate from those at plate boundaries, they will have developed labels that let them understand the significance of the New Madrid events. They would understand, just as an audience understands what Medea is doing backstage, without the need to make things explicit.

Telling students how a study was done does not tell them what thought processes were going on during the study. It does not indicate how the person doing the work was changed by doing it. If you agree that active mental participation on the part of students is necessary for effective learning, you can devise activities to get your students doing things in ways analogous to how you learn about things, which comment leads to the next quotation.

> "Research then, should provide practitioners, not just
> with findings in the form of activities or behaviors
> that work but ways of thinking and empirical premises
> related to teaching and learning."
> **V. Richardson**

The author of the quote is saying don't tell me how you do something; tell me what principle you are addressing. This is good advice because it is highly likely that the technique you use will not work for me because our students and our personalities differ. But if I think the principle is worth dealing with, I will develop a way to address it that is compatible with my situation.

After I read the article from which this quotation came I stopped writing "How I do it" articles for education journals. If the reader notes an inconsistency with the previous section (which is a "How I would do it" discussion), I will invoke a comment attributed to Walt Whitman, namely: "Do I contradict myself? Very well, I contradict myself."

*"...(The) relevant unit of meaning for the translator is
not the word, but the message..."*
Michael Moerman

Substitute the word teacher for translator and the fellow is saying that *what one says* in a lecture is not as important as *what is conveyed*. Think about what kind of messages we want students to receive? Are we more concerned with making sure that the structure of our presentation is logically correct, or are we concerned that they understand the meta-messages in the material. That is, do we want them to understand:

What was determined? That is, the facts, results, etc..

What was done? The steps needed to find the results.

Why the study was done? The need to frame a context.

Why students should be interested? Create a more specific context.

Typically, we do the first of the items on this list, and sometimes the second. But we often assume that students will understand, implicitly, the others.

We all have expectations about how the world works: that is, how things are done and how other people will behave. For example, we can drive in traffic reasonably safely because we have learned to judge distances and relative velocities, so when we see a car coming toward us, we know if it is safe to make a turn in front of it.

We function in society because of a variety of analogous expectations. We assign situations to known categories, and once that is done, we know how to deal with them. Recognizing common features (patterns) provides us with strategies. Stories represent a good example. When we watch a program on television, say a mystery, we are familiar with the conventions of that kind of story, so we have a mental model of what is going on, a model that differs from one we use for situation comedies. In both cases we infer what is going to happen next based on our mental model of the program.

But what happens to students in an academic environment? They are flooded with new information, information that is presented using new vocabularies. Most of the material is abstract, with only a weak correspondence to the things they experience in life.

It is difficult for instructors who have internalized the details of their disciplines to be aware of the reasons students might not understand what is going on in a class. Is the vocabulary completely foreign to them? Is the logic obscure? The fact that you are speaking the same language as the students does not mean that they understand *why* you are saying *what* you are saying.

How do different people respond to a lecture? It depends on their tacit knowledge of the subject.

If I listen to a lecture on earthquakes I will recognize how the lecturer has organized the material. I might think: "this approach is interesting but I would have done it in a different way."

A graduate student might think: "that is a good way to explain this topic. I will use this approach tomorrow when the subject comes up in my recitation section.

Undergraduate students will normally be trying, perhaps desperately, to write down what appear to be important statements. Students have many decisions to make regarding how much detail to include in their notes; relationships between ideas rarely are perceived unless they are expressly mentioned.

Prior experience determines the differences between these reactions. I have a degree in Geophysics and taught about earthquakes for many years. The graduate student may (but not necessarily) have taken one course on earthquakes. Unless the undergraduates live in California, they may know nothing about them, and even those from California may not know much. Once I gave an assignment on rain forests to a class which included a woman from Brazil. She said she knew no more about rain forests than the other students because she had always lived in cities.

Prior experience determines how much tacit knowledge one has about a subject, and tacit knowledge underlies our conversations with other people. The more you have the more likely you will respond to new material with "top-down" (knowledge-driven) processes. If you have little knowledge, you will be limited to "bottom-up" processes, which are more time-consuming. So communication between experts and neophytes is not always effective because their labeling of the information about the topic is vastly different.

Yekovitch and Walker discussed the importance of tacit knowledge by showing how it underlies our routine conversations. They gave the following example:

"They called to make a reservation."

What the example really says is:

They (customers) called (on the telephone) (to someone) (at a restaurant [place where customers can purchase and be served meals]) to make a reservation (arrangement to hold a table for one's use).

A geological example might be:

Those who live in floodplains endanger themselves and impose costs on the community.

This statement really says:

Those (residents) who live in floodplains (places where the water level is subject to large changes in elevation) endanger themselves (subject themselves to death by drowning) and impose costs (money to rebuild or relocate structures) on the community (the political entity to which they pay taxes and from which they expect services).

In each case the details are connected by a network of implicit knowledge, a network which is context-dependent. So interpreting a terse statement requires top-down processing that involves familiarity with the culture. These are simple examples, but to what extent is an adequate interpretation of what you say in class dependent on these kinds of networks of tacit knowledge?

"If a lion could talk we could not understand him."
Wittgenstein, *Philosophical Investigations*

This comment is part of Wittgenstein's discussion on how the way we speak affects and is affected by what we can know about the world. Taking the statement literally, an animal's sensory experiences differ markedly from ours. For example, the sense of smell is much more highly developed in animals than in us, so the sensory input to the brain of a lion is not at all comparable to that of a human. In addition, the "wiring" of the brain of a lion differs markedly from that in a human brain. The differentiation of structure in the left and right hemispheres in human brains resulted in the ability to do things that even other primates cannot do, such as throwing things accurately and learning Calculus. So the combination of an animal's sensory experiences and the data processing that occurs in its brain will result in "concepts" that probably could not be articulated in a way that we could understand, even if the lion could express them verbally.

Wittgenstein used the statement about the lion as a metaphor for communications between people of different cultures. In the paragraphs preceding the statement quoted he said that even if we speak the language of people in a strange country with strange customs, we could never really completely understand the people and we could not know the reasons why we could not (a double whammy).

As an Austrian teaching at Cambridge University in Great Britain, Wittgenstein may have been relating personal experiences.

Earlier in the book he said that we use the "common behavior of mankind" to interpret the activities of strangers, but he clearly thought that that is not sufficient because this common behavior is a small subset of the activities undertaken by people. He felt that the overlap of the ways people of different cultures think would be too small to allow understanding. The fact that they do and say some things that we do is not, he felt, sufficient to enable us to understand everything they do. Returning to the metaphor of the lion, the overlap of common experiences between us and a lion would be essentially zero, and the overlap between us and people from a different culture would be finite, but still too small he felt, to allow complete understanding.

Wittgenstein may have been exaggerating to make a point (about different human cultures, not about the lion) but Clifford Geertz wrote similar things about the years he spent doing ethnographic work in Indonesia and Morocco. He did not confine himself to merely describing actions and events; he did his best to put them in the context of the particular culture he was studying. But he was not convinced he ever really "got to the bottom" of those cultures. And Michael Agar gave another example of how difficult it is to understand people of other cultures. An American living in Austria, he was fluent in spoken German. Yet quite often he was not sure when speaking to someone whether he should use the personal or impersonal form of the pronoun "you." In fact, his entire book is devoted to the difficulties that different languacultures" cause for those attempting to communicate in another language. A fascinating book!

As another independent verification of Wittgenstein's point, I once took a subscription to the weekly edition of a newspaper from Great Britain, *The Manchester Guardian*. On a few occasions I tried to do the crossword puzzles, but could not fill in a single word. Although written in English, the clues were culture-dependent so they meant nothing to me.

> "In recent centuries, we speakers of this lovely language
> have reduced the English verb almost entirely to
> the indicative mood. But beneath that specious and
> arrogant assumption of certainty all the ancient,
> cloudy, moody powers and options of the subjunctive
> remain in force."
> **Ursula Le Guin (1989)**

She goes on to say that using the indicative is equivalent to pointing your finger at your experiences, whereas the subjunctive joins them using analogy, probability, contingency, etc. The subjunctive is the foundation of narrative. It lets us link events from the past, the future, or in some faraway land. Contrast the language in the U.S. Constitution with that in the Declaration of Independence. One document defines a form of government, the other provides the narrative justifying a change in government. One is suitable for legal discussions, the other provides the cultural cement that helps hold the nation together, in a manner analogous to the "Coyote" tales told in the Hopi tradition.

McCloskey discussed the same point by distinguishing between using a model to explain a phenomenon and using a story. He noted that if someone doing science or economics uses a model successfully, the result will be equations with simple solutions. On the other hand, a story about the phenomenon can often explain it equally well. Most economics textbooks use models in the form of equations and graphs to explain a point. But the book by Rivoli examines the nature of the global economy by telling a story about how T-shirts are made. She traced the passage of the material from the cotton grown in Texas to the fabric and then the shirts made in China to the Outlet stores in America where the shirts are sold. It provides a complementary approach to the standard way of teaching about globalization.

> "What we cannot speak about we must pass over in silence."
> **Wittgenstein,** *Tractatus Logico Philosophicus*

This is the last proposition in Wittgenstein's first book. At first glance the statement seems to be a tautology, but if we revise it slightly, to the form "What we cannot speak about we cannot communicate," it makes sense. Think of the feelings produced by music. How can I convey my impressions of a cello concerto by Bach or a symphony by Mozart to someone else? William James once wrote that music gives us ontological information. It is not apparent to me how one could effectively articulate ontological information. My mother was an artist. She was never pleased with photographs of her paintings, because what the camera recorded never quite corresponded to what she "saw." Perhaps those who wish to convey the nature of ontological information need to think more in terms of the subjunctive. Analogy, probability, contingency.

In the preface to his three-volume set of "introductory" Physics textbooks, Richard Feynman wrote that he did not think that the courses (on which the books were based) were a success because he felt that too few students understood the material at the level that he expected. That is surprising, because the students were Freshmen at Cal Tech. Where could we expect to find better science students? Perhaps Feynman was not aware of what tacit knowledge was needed for his students to understand the material at the level he expected.

Students may not "know" something because they cannot call upon the networks of tacit knowledge required to understand the professor. And professors may not realize that they are not communicating because they assume that everyone is a member of their "community" and so can speak their language.

How does learning affect us?

> "O chestnut tree, great-rooted blossomer,
> Are you the leaf, the blossom or the bole?
> O body swayed to music, O brightening glance,
> How shall we know the dancer from the dance?"
> **W. B. Yeats**

This question has been used by writers in different ways. Ursula Le Guin (2004) used it to end a discussion of how one's personality affects one's life and how one's life affects one's personality. To her, life clearly is a dialectic experience. As the dancer performs the dance, his/her past experiences affect the performance, just as the performance changes the dancer.

Pamela McCorduck used the concept illustrated by the question in the quotation to discuss the effect of literacy on society. She noted that literate people can experience much more about the modern world than illiterate ones because literate people can accumulate the experiences of society in general. Their memories contain "chunks" of information about the world that are cross-referenced as they accumulate. That is, when we learn something new we relate it to what we already know. So the information is changed as it is learned, just as the person who learns the information is changed by the learning. As the person changes, the manner in which he/she reacts to future sources of information also changes - manner referring to mental processes.

Note the similarity between these uses of the quotation and Roger Schank's comments on how memories develop by assigning labels to our experiences. He noted that assigning labels is not straightforward because it requires a process of deconstruction and reconstruction. Memory storage involves revising what we hear and read. You tell me something and I take it apart and tuck the parts away in my memory. In that process, I associate the components of your story to things in my past experience be assigning labels to them. When I feel called upon to respond to something that you or someone else says, I use the labels to choose my response. This is why different people respond differently to the world around them.

The process of creating semantic memories is analogous to the digestion of food. The proteins we consume are broken down into their constituent parts - the amino acids. Then sequences of the amino acids are strung together to form new proteins, the ones we need. The labels we assign to the components of a story determine which components are strung together at some later time. In effect, Schank thinks of memory in terms of a relational data base, consisting of sets of memories that are cross-indexed in various ways. The more entries a memory has in the index, the more likely we are to call upon it for a response, so the ability to recall something depends on the number of associations it has.

Unfortunately, this discussion is missing something. I wish I knew how to help students go through the deconstruction and labeling process. However *I* do it seems to be buried too deeply for me to articulate it to others. It would appear that the only way to learn to do it is to do it. Recall the quote by Antonio Machado that began this chapter.

When learning something complex, the beginner must become proficient in a performing a variety of tasks, and the sequence in which they must be done. Eventually, repetition provides mastery of each task and, in my experience, at that point the significance of the sequence becomes apparent, so the student can see how the tasks are related to each other. That insight provides an understanding of the entire operation. A beginning graduate student does these things when learning to do research by working in a laboratory. At first the reasons for doing certain things are a bit obscure because the jargon of the particular specialty is not really understood. Eventually, the tasks, their sequence, and their relationships to everything else in the laboratory are understood, and the student can begin to do original work. Unfortunately, undergraduates rarely have the opportunity to work through this kind of process.

> "In every point of this city you can, in turn, sleep, make tools, cook, accumulate gold, disrobe, reign, sell, question oracles. The traveler roams all around and has nothing but doubts: he is unable to distinguish the features of the city."
> **Italo Calvino**

Without a framework to identify what is happening there is no way to know what is happening. If every district in a city is identical, if the activities occurring on every street are the same, we could never know where we were. In describing this imagined city Calvino tells us that nature does not have categories; we impose them on nature so we can function.

Wandering eastward in the lower parts of Manhattan Island, leaving Tribeca, one passes through "Chinatown," to the Lower East Side (in which most of the signs are in Hebrew). Travelers have no difficulty knowing where they are because we have assigned labels to the areas in various ways.

What about lectures? How many teachers structure their lectures so that students are aware of the categories underlying the material that is presented? That is, aware of the categories to the extent that they recognize the differences between "neighborhoods?" It is not enough to tell students what the categories are; they will just write down the words and assume that they are part of the content of the lecture. Do your students really understand the difference between the content of the lecture and its structure? We tend to assume that students recognize the patterns underlying what we say, and use those patterns in responding to questions and assignments. We usually do not expect undergraduates to suggest significant and interesting revisions of the standard patterns, but how often do we examine how they actually use what we give them? That is, how often do we examine their work on its own merits, rather than compare their approach with what we have presented to them?

Clearly, we cannot make that kind of distinction with multiple-choice tests. The task is a bit easier with essay tests, but in that case we have to wade through how students say things, and they hardly ever write coherent paragraphs. We need ways to learn how they think. Judging students on normal assignments is not always useful because the evaluation is a comparison with the "standard model." It is a measure of how well they have learned the material in the lectures, but it is not necessarily a measure of how they *think* about the subject.

Another problem that complicates teaching and learning is due to an attitude fostered by university administrators for the last 50 or so years - namely that the best teachers are those who are actively doing research in their fields of interest. Since the creation of the National Science Foundation, in the early 1950s, and later of the National Institutes of Health, funds for scientific research (and for the overhead costs associated with the research) have poured into the universities. Since then, average class sizes have increased and faculty teaching loads have decreased (because putting more students in a class results in fewer sections that have to be taught). Economies of scale are usually invoked to justify these trends, but the real reason is to give faculty time to do the research that brings in the federal grants.

The shift away from teaching has also been justified by the belief that spillovers from the research that faculty do is an essential part of the courses they taught. The claim is that students are bound to benefit when they are taught by faculty doing "cutting edge" research in their fields. If faculty cannot provide up-to-date information on their specialties unless they are engaged in "cutting edge" research, the clear implication is that to be good at teaching, one must also be doing research. This belief then developed into the myth that one who is good at research is necessarily good at teaching. There is nothing but anecdotal evidence for these beliefs, but they are commonly used to justify a management system that puts research ahead of teaching, in order to receive external funding from government grants.

Before going on, I will agree that it is possible that the instructor doing research in a discipline can interact more effectively with students in the advanced courses in a curriculum than someone who is not doing research (but I will mention an exception later). The students in advanced courses have acquired some of the tacit knowledge needed to understand the point of the course and the points made by the instructor. But most of the students taking an introductory science course are doing so to satisfy a graduation requirement, not because they plan to major in the subject. They have no tacit knowledge to allow them to interpret what they are being told, so the personalities of the instructors may have more of an effect on students' opinions of the course than their research credentials.

To make a categorical statement that those who are good at research are also good at teaching (without specifying the courses taught) is to say that teaching involves little more than conveying current information. Proponents of this position justify it by claiming that the person doing research understands the subject better than those not involved with research and can, therefore, explain it more clearly.

The fallacy in that assertion should be obvious. No single aspect of a discipline dominates an introductory science course, and no one can do research in all areas of a discipline, so it follows that no one can explain all aspects of a field more clearly than anyone else, merely because he or she is active in research.

But let's consider some examples. According to the British Physicist Horace Lamb, one of his teachers, James Clerk Maxwell, gave terrible lectures. Maxwell apparently never prepared for a lecture, so he made lots of mistakes on the blackboard. But Lamb said that he learned more physics watching Maxwell correct his mistakes than he did from any textbook because he learned how a genius thought about the subject. Unfortunately, few of us have that kind of experience. On the other hand, an example of a gifted research scientist who could also be a good teacher is the Nobel laureate Richard Feynman. The three-volume set of "introductory" Physics books made from tapes of his lectures is outstanding, so the lectures themselves must have been fascinating. But Feynman taught the courses only once; he would not waste his time doing them again. And according to one of his biographers, Feynman resisted teaching the courses for several years because he avoided teaching responsibilities whenever possible. So we have one genius who was a terrible teacher and another who could have been excellent at teaching if only he had been willing to teach.

Those who claim that one must be good at research to be good at teaching may really be saying that the enthusiasm conveyed by those doing research is contagious and is quite likely to instill in students an interest in doing science. That position is easier to defend, but it implies that those who do not do research are not enthusiastic about what they teach.

Consider a counterexample. In the late 1970s, a few years before he retired, I met a Geologist who had taught at one of the SUNY colleges in New York State for his entire career. An account of his dissertation research was the only journal article he ever published, and he never applied for research grant funds from any government agency. Clearly, he considered himself a teacher. Yet when I met him, he was aware of some papers I had published that were peripherally related to one of the advanced courses he taught, and he was familiar with the literature on the subject in general. So, although he did no research, he read the literature that pertained to his area of interest, and presumably, discussed aspects of it in his classes. His students considered him to be an outstanding teacher. A number of them went on to graduate school and I know of two who received Ph.D. degrees in areas related to his specialty. Can anyone say that he was not a good teacher? Anecdotal arguments work both ways.

A reasonable person might assume that those who are hired by universities are expected to teach. If that is a misconception, the schools should be clear about the matter to the legislators and parents who fund the schools.

But for the moment, assume that the best researchers *are* the best teachers. In that case, surely university administrators would take advantage of this relationship and assign the best teachers to teach all of the introductory science courses. Those with large research grants, who clearly are the best at what they do, would be teaching introductory courses with hundreds of students, most of them non-science majors. No graduate students would be filling in for the professors; the full time faculty would be doing all the work and inspiring a generation of students.

Does anyone believe that the research-oriented faculty would put up with that? When would they do the work proposed in their grant proposals if they are spending their time working with hundreds of non-science majors?

> "...the question is: How...can a person today get himself to do something which he had not been able to do yesterday, or last year? How can competencies, abilities and skills develop?"
> **Gilbert Ryle**

Do such skills develop when you listen to an expert explain them? If so, the belief that someone skilled in research is necessarily a good teacher may be true. But consider this example that Ryle gives. To compose a sonnet you must follow certain rules. You must have 14 lines, a certain rhyme scheme, and a certain meter. A teacher can give you those rules but you have to use them to do something new.

The rules represent a set of prohibitions. They seem to constrain you, but in obeying them you have the freedom to innovate. For example, Ryle notes that the rule "keep off the grass" lets you walk anywhere else, whereas the rule "stay on the walk" leaves you little freedom. If the rules permit experimentation, and your work satisfies them you will have written an original sonnet. If the rules specify "do it this way," your result will not be creative.

Regardless of how good you are at studying mountain ranges, or sequencing genes, you cannot make a scientist out of a student merely by explaining the rules: you must let the student *use* the rules in ways that are appropriate for the discipline. A person learns by doing a thing and improves by trying to do it better each time. This is how graduate students learn to become scientists. But students in introductory courses do not get that sort of attention, so one has to wonder how much they learn.

Learning involves what the students do, not what the teachers say they themselves did.

Are academic skills transferable? The fact that students do not seem to use what they learn in one course when they take another course may be due to the fact that we do not structure the material properly. In introductory science courses we tend to tell students about things, rather than giving them ways to work out answers for themselves. The main problem is that in a science course students do not learn the material in the same way that they learn things that are important to them - i.e. in situated learning experiences.

Students do not learn to do text messaging in a formal classroom setting. They are immersed in the newest video game or cell phone technologies in ways not possible in an academic curriculum. Academic learning rarely is "situated" in ways that students find meaningful.

Isolating actions from their contexts (as it is done in traditionally taught courses) facilitates analysis, but it also masks much of the meaning of the activities. To use a simple example, a right fielder throws a baseball to the second baseman to keep a runner on first, whereas a quarterback throws a football to a receiver in the end zone to score a touchdown. The physics underlying the paths of the balls is largely the same, although the reasons for throwing the balls differ markedly.

The context of an action tells us *why* something was done, whereas an analysis of the motion involved merely tells us *how* it occurred. To some extent, to value knowledge separated from its context by analyzing activities as ends in themselves, is to de-value cultural continuity.

People learn in every society, but only in western societies is learning done in formats that are removed from the society's culture. Of course, there are good reasons for separating education and culture. One is the abstract nature of the content of many subjects taught in the schools. You can learn something about fluid mechanics by building and sailing boats. But there is a limit to how far experiential knowledge can take us. Design of hulls intended to function under new conditions requires scientific principles, not techniques handed down over generations. A society that is largely separated from nature, as are all western societies today, cannot function without manufactured products that are the result of technical education that is not possible to hand down as is done in traditional societies.

In a traditional society it is easy to determine who has learned the lessons taught to all. If your canoe overturns in moderately rough water you must have deviated from the traditional teachings, and the deviation must not have been worthwhile. A navigator faced with the task of guiding a canoe from one island the size of a western shopping mall to another small island a few hundred miles away, needs to know how the task has been done in the past. He must spend years learning how to use information about the stars, waves, and currents to determine where he is at any given time. The efforts are not confined to rote memorization: discussions with South Sea navigators by Gladwin suggest that Schank's overlay process may be involved. Those who learn the lessons well usually reach the other island.

But this approach does not reward attempts at innovation. And, if the lessons involve abstract material (*e.g.* integrating a function using the principles of Calculus) it is not as easy to determine whether the student can use the material effectively. One can construct tests that represent the manner in which the material was discussed in class, but being able to reproduce a skill in a formal class setting is not the same as knowing how and when to use the skill in a real-life situation. The canoe builder and the navigator learn in the context in which the material learned will be used. But in western societies the contexts change so rapidly that the teacher of Calculus cannot possibly know how and when the students will be asked to do something that involves the skills learned in class. Instruction in our society is made as abstract as possible because it is intended to be applicable to very general situations. And because it is abstract, it is not internalized as effectively as what you learn by watching and helping your father shape the hull of a canoe or by helping your older brother tune the engine of his car.

Learning in the "real world" is a long-term, largely self-paced and unconscious process that provides people with what is needed to fit into our (mostly) suburban and urban culture. We learn things such as how to conduct financial transactions, how to behave at public meetings, how to deal with noisy neighbors, and how to succeed at our jobs. Much of this kind of learning is accomplished by mimicking what we see others do and by actually doing the tasks required by our respective cultures. Initially, we flounder and require directions, but eventually, we develop a "big picture" of the tasks, one that gives us the confidence we need to succeed at them.

Learning by modifying existing memories differs markedly from the learning that is involved in our formal educational system, in which students are not allowed the luxury of adapting slowly over time. In school, students are expected to assimilate over relatively short time spans abstract information that is usually presented to them orally, by means of a specialized vocabulary. The setting is artificial and the material is presented to them quickly, because the schedule requires that new topics be introduced fairly regularly. The academic model of learning differs markedly from that by which students have learned everything else in their lives, so it should not be surprising that students usually are not easily able to develop a functional understanding of an assigned project.

> "An algorithm is a procedure for solving a problem that guarantees (or claims to guarantee) an answer."
> **Pamela McCorduck**

The use of an algorithm involves a finite number of steps and works only on problems that do not change as they are being solved. The algorithmic approach presupposes that the problem can be specified precisely and that an algorithm that is appropriate exists.

Consider the No Child Left Behind legislation as an algorithm intended to solve the nation's educational problems. Can it possibly be effective? To answer that question, consider the following ones:

Is the real problem well-defined?

Does the legislation target the real problem?

Is the real problem sufficiently static that an algorithmic approach is appropriate?

Without answers to these questions, no one can be sure of the efficacy of the legislation.

"What you will find missing from..(proposals for large-scale changes in a system) are any prophecies about what will go wrong, what mistakes will be made, or what negative consequences will arise from it. These considerations are absent because ...(prophets) create plans based on oversimplified assumptions and one-dimensional metaphors."
Neil Postman (1976)

Once again, think of the No Child Left Behind legislation, which is based on the assumption that, substandard performance of students on standardized tests is due solely to poor teaching, so the solution to the problem is to identify which teachers should be fired and which schools should be closed. The legislation cannot possibly result in an improvement in the education of students because monitoring average grades on standardized tests provides no insight on how to improve learning. Federal administrators do not seem to understand that the problems with the educational system today are caused by the nature of the system, not by the quality of the teachers, or the existence of teachers' unions. Federal administrators should be required to read W. Edwards Deming's works on quality control.

Must we be efficient in order to be effective?

It is not efficient to spend time stimulating collaboration between students - i.e. having students working together in a social setting. It is much more efficient to lecture to large groups of students and give standardized tests. But if the social aspect of learning is rejected in the name of efficiency, something important is lost. A student is much more likely to understand what another student does not understand than an instructor is. Student teaching student is not efficient but it is effective because it is "more situated" than is a lecture.

Efficiency involves putting means before ends. Emphasizing the importance of an efficient means removes the entire process from a social setting. The means that are the most efficient are the favored ones. That is basically the economic argument that says that the best approach to something is the one that gives the highest yield (measured in some economic sense). It puts cost-effective teaching methods ahead of learning.

It is easy to teach a class: we do it all the time. But to teach students we cannot rely just on presenting information and testing recall of the material. It is not adequate to say that the goal is for the students to get "better grades." After all:

What does "better" mean? And what do grades indicate?

The words "better grades" imply that higher scores on tests correlate with understanding of the material presented in class. That, in turn, requires the assumption that the tests are really diagnostic of what the students understand and of what the instructor wants them to know. But how many teachers are experts in designing tests?

Forget about tests and grades. To really teach students we need to know something about the students; otherwise, whatever we do is not likely to work. The more we know about them the more likely we will be able to determine what to do in order to be successful.

It does not matter how hard you work if you are doing the wrong things.

Students' performances vary considerably, so if we want to teach them in ways that will help them to learn, we need to address the causes of the variations. A partial list of causes that I think most people would agree with includes:

poor study habits

poor math skills

poor reading skills

not enough time to spend on the course (e.g. working at a job for too many hours.)

Will the traditional methods of improving teaching deal with these problems? If I change my style by telling jokes, showing more movies, asking more questions during the class, giving more short assignments, etc., will I overcome these problems? Not likely, because the changes we usually adopt are aimed at the symptoms (lack of interest), not the causes. The only way to deal with these problems is to somehow deal directly with the causes. Browsing through W. Edwards Deming's book on quality control is a useful exercise for a teacher who wants ideas about how effective changes can be accomplished. But one should concentrate on his discussions of stable and unstable industrial systems, not on the sections on teaching - he taught only Ph.D. students.

We judge students based on how well they conform to the existing system, rather than asking how the system could be changed so they would develop a better understanding of the material. The Economist John Kenneth Galbraith once said that given the choice between making a major change in their approach to something and proving that a change is not necessary, most people immediately sit down and begin to work on the proof.

At this point it seems useful to consider some of the ideas mentioned about learning at a more fundamental level. Learning involves processing information and then storing it in one's memory. But what is "memory?" Francis Crick spent a number of years in the field of neuroscience. He and a colleague concentrated on the visual system in the brain because they felt that they could specify an experimental approach to understanding how that aspect of the brain worked more easily than for other areas of neuroscience. Some of the things he wrote about vision provide a useful way to think about learning. The following statement from one of his books (Crick, 1994) is an example.

> "...(Vision) is a constructive process in which the brain
> responds in parallel to many different 'features' of
> the visual scene and attempts to combine them into
> meaningful wholes, using its past experience as a guide.
> Seeing involves active processes in your brain that lead
> to an explicit multilevel, symbolic interpretation of the
> visual scene."

Crick noted that when we see something we seem to have a picture in our head - a picture of the scene before us. But there is no screen in the brain that produces patterns of light corresponding to the visual world. A useful analogy for what happens involves storage of data in a computer. An image stored in a computer's memory is not actually stored there as a picture. Instead, electrical charges are stored in the memory chips in the form of an array of numbers, each one representing the light intensity at some point in the image. What is stored in memory does not look like a picture, but the computer can produce the picture on its screen on demand.

The brain must do something equivalent to that kind of storage. It must take the values of light intensity sent to it from the retina of the eye, produce a symbolic description of them at some higher level and have a way to link the two, just as a computer's software links the electrical charges with the array of numbers.

In the case of the computer there is a one-to-one relationship between the array of numbers and the electrical charges, but in the brain, the relationship has to be much more complex because the representation of the visual signals is partly based on our past experience. For example, if the visual scene that produced the signals is a street in a city, the symbolic representation created might convey "city" to me and "the neighborhood" to you. The visual scene is the same for you and for me, but the associations made by our brains will be affected by our different experiences, which often leads to confusion in conversations.

So it seems that the memories already stored symbolically in one's brain affect the manner in which new representations are created. Thus, the firing of neurons creates the representation that correlates with some aspect of the visual world, but that representation must also be affected by one's previous experiences with that aspect of the world (more on the word "must" later).

The relationship between the ideas in the last few paragraphs and the model of memory suggested by Roger Schank should be clear, but I am reminded of a joke that is relevant here.

> An instructor in a mathematics class told his students that he was not going to prove the next theorem in the text because the proof was obvious. Then he said aloud: "Wait, is it really obvious?" After spending several minutes thinking about it, he said to the class, "Yes, the proof is obvious."

So in case it is not obvious, I will say a bit more. The relationship between what one sees today and one's previous experiences is the link between the visual system and the learning of material. When I read something in a book my brain interprets the visual signals as described above. The signals are converted into symbolic representations that are meaningful to me. Those representations (letters strung together) are converted into new representations that we call "words," which are themselves used to construct other representations we call sentences. If I cannot read, the construction process will stop at the visual level (the group of letters). If I *can* read, the higher order representations will be constructed because they will be meaningful to me.

If I "understand" these various strings, it is because my brain has taken the symbolic representations produced in the visual system and constructed new, higher order representations, comparing them with "neural correlates" (Crick's term) that resulted from this process in the past. So the firing of neurons correlating with previously learned material from Chemistry will be "consulted" when the firing of neurons correlating with new material about the water molecule occurs (Recall Roger Schank's concept of "semantic memory"). If the comparison were not made, a person's memory would consist of a string of unconnected "statements." We might "know" a lot but we would "understand" nothing. Hence the use of the word "must" earlier.

This seems to be a way to use Crick's ideas about how the brain works to explain how one learns and how (semantic) memories are constructed. Of course, the details of how and where those neural correlations are stored, and how they interact with others is not clear. But, as the saying goes, that is another story.

EPILOGUE

It seems useful now to re-emphasize the distinction between the short-term educational activities that go on in public schools, colleges and universities, and the long-term education that results from living a life. The school-based activities are intense, and because of that, can be quite effective. The life-long activities are largely subliminal and are effective because they are repetitive and "situated" in our experiences.

Perhaps the most complete description of the long-term educational experience was given by Henry Adams in his autobiography. Adams was not satisfied with any of the components of his education: the formal educational training he received at Harvard College (class of 1858); the experiences gained by living in Germany for two years; the experiences he received by working as secretary to the Ambassador (his father) at the U.S. Embassy in London during the Civil War; and the experience gained by teaching history at Harvard in the latter part of the Century. He felt that each of these components was basically a capsule; no single one of them was sufficient in itself, but collectively, they all contributed to the end result.

Adams would not have been receptive to the kind of teaching that stresses the importance of covering as much content as possible. Based on his writings, he would have recognized that no course (or even a degree program) was as important to one's education as the subliminal effects of one's overall experiences. I suspect that he would be receptive to the idea that learning is a much more subtle concept than most people realize.

TECHNOLOGY IN EDUCATION

"Equo ne credite"
Aeneid, II, 48

Laocoon's warning to the Trojans, which was ignored, provides a good introduction to the topic of using technology in education. One does not have to be a Luddite to think that the claims made by proponents of technology may be exaggerated, and that instructors should be cautious about adopting new tools merely because they are new. In fact, the skeptical attitude is fairly common; proponents of new technologies complain that relatively few instructors are willing to experiment with their courses by adopting new approaches. Why are some instructors reluctant to adopt these innovations? Perhaps they are aware that the appropriate use of educational technologies must be focused; that some of the approaches proposed may do many things well, but those things may not be what the instructors want to do.

A sensible person does not automatically adopt a new technology before asking some questions. Two fundamentally different questions come to mind.

Will a new technology allow you to do what you want to do?

55

Or will it merely let you do something you cannot do now?

The distinction is important. To answer the first question you must have clearly defined goals. You must recognize that what you are doing now is not sufficient and that you could do a better job if you had a certain capability. I wrote a 10 page manual on how to teach the on-line course I was developing without mentioning explicitly which electronic "tools" I was going to use to implement the course. Once I knew exactly what I wanted to do, I consulted with a technical support person to find out which software tools were available for each component of the course. As evidence that the tools were not nearly as important as the things the tools had to do, consider that from time to time, as I taught the course, I had to find substitutes for some of the tools that had become unavailable for one reason or another.

The second question is easier to answer: just ask the proponents of a new technology what it can do. They will give you a list from which you can extract items that may be of interest to you. Having people hand you a tool is convenient, and even helpful, if some of the capabilities are compatible with your goals. But unless that compatibility exists the benefit to your students may be small. And if the tool will not necessarily benefit your students, why adopt it? Just because you cannot do something now is not a good reason to do it when it becomes possible.

The semester after I started teaching my on-line course, the university announced that a team from the Information Technology support staff had developed an elaborate course management software package that would facilitate putting courses on-line. The system seemingly could do everything an instructor normally did in a traditionally-taught course in a classroom. Among other things, it allowed an instructor to post assignments and readings, it administered and graded quizzes, it kept track of students' grades, and it provided an e-mail system for communicating with the students. Of course, everyone was encouraged to use the package.

I did not use the new system, partly because I did not need many of the components it provided, and partly because I saw no reason to change my course to make it fit someone else's expectations of how an on-line course should be taught. "Let a thousand flowers bloom" was my belief. In addition, I recognized that:

Those who developed the system were not concerned with what students were learning. Their goal was to develop a system that would make instructors feel comfortable.

The system was intended to map a traditional lecture course into an on-line format in as close to a one-to-one relationship as possible. The logic behind this approach was sound: If instructors thought that the system would allow them to do the things they normally did, they would be more likely to use the system, even if they were not entirely comfortable with on-line teaching. And (need I mention it?) the more the system was used, the better the technical support team would look.

But a one-to-one mapping is a recipe for disaster. I was not interested in doing the things I had done in the traditional classroom. I felt that the on-line environment would let me discard much of what *I normally did*, so that I could concentrate on *what the students were doing*.

My course worked because having decided what I wanted the students to do, I chose components of available technologies that would allow them to do it, and which would allow me to monitor how well they did it. That last phrase is important. I could monitor the student achievement without the use of standardized tests.

Of course, it was comforting to know that although some administrators frowned at my reluctance to adopt something new, I did not have to worry that, like Laocoon, I would be dragged into the sea and devoured by serpents.

The development of an infrastructure facilitates the use of technology in teaching, but its existence alone tells us nothing useful about what is happening on a campus. Fiber-optic lines, broadband communications, wireless technology, abundant software, training centers, etc. do not guarantee that students will learn anything, much less anything new or useful.

But putting a blackboard in every classroom changed education. It was a revolutionary move because it changed the way instructors presented material and, by having students work out things at the board, it gave instructors a way to see clearly how well how or poorly students understood the material.

I still recall standing at the blackboard in a high school Latin class 55 years ago. The teacher certainly was aware of how little I knew about the subjunctive mood.

The level of this technology was such that instructors and students could use it immediately because there was no learning curve. And different instructors could use it as they wished - to post important items, derive equations, have students work individually, etc.

The blackboard was an ideal technology because it was easy to use, it supported several kinds of activities, and the only way it could break down was if you ran out of chalk. The overhead projector was just a minor improvement over the blackboard. It let the material be seen by more students, and one could show illustrations in color (even though the students took notes in black and white), but this change was not revolutionary. And Power Point presentations are just electronic versions of what is done with the overhead projector. They are convenient for the instructor, but provide nothing new for the students.

It is not clear to me to what extent the electronic technologies have changed education. But the potential for change does exist. Spread sheets, data bases, and graphic and statistical software packages enable a student to examine data sets in ways not feasible before. So the potential for active learning exists, and the level of analysis one can expect from students should be higher than in the past. But the level at which these tools are introduced is important. It does not seem realistic to ask students in introductory courses to analyze data sets using sophisticated software packages. We cannot expect students to make use of tools that enable analysis of a subject until they know something about the subject.

Of course new technologies will remain "on the shelf" until faculty see their potential. That means either that the faculty consist of "early adopters," or that we wait a generation so that students who grow up using the different technologies become faculty members who take the new ideas for granted.

The mere existence of a technology does not give me a pedagogical reason to use it. Just being able to do something more rapidly may not be not enough to justify the cost and time involved in doing something new.If students will learn more quickly and deeply, that is sufficient reason. But using something because it is flashy is not.

Some of the electronic technologies facilitate delivery of content. They make it possible to "teach" more students at a time, to teach students at widely scattered sites, and to present material in more ways. The emphasis is on how to deliver material efficiently to more people at a time. Cost effectiveness is a god.

But less is said about how students receive the information, or how the technology changes them from passive recipients to active learners. Learning is not listening to lectures and taking exams, nor is it reading books and writing papers. Learning involves acquiring information and transforming it according to one's background and goals. It requires digestion as well as reception.

Will a technology help me see something in a new way? Or recognize its relevance to something else? The instructor who derives equations on a blackboard shows students the logic underlying mathematics. Students see how certain tools (e.g. the binomial theorem) are used to simplify expressions to achieve a goal. The students are not doing new work on their own, but they see how someone else did it once before. And they *see* it. They get more than the words: they see how to use the theorem and the result of using it. They achieve a goal (the answer) and they store in their memories a context for the use of the tool that provided the answer.

Whenever a new technology provides that kind of experience, it will be adopted.

Whenever we consider using a new technology we should wonder what kinds of things we can do with it.

- Does it allow us to do something new? The blackboard allows us to display the logic of a discipline.

- Does it allow us to do something we normally do, only more easily? The overhead projector allows us to display lecture notes and precisely drawn illustrations to a large class.

- Or does it merely allow us to do something ordinary, but in a flashy manner? Power-point presentations are convenient for the speaker but do not represent an innovation in teaching or learning.

Trading in my sedan for a convertible may change my image but it provides no improvement in meeting my transportation needs.

"...as our ability to manipulate numbers with...(a computer) became more sophisticated, we wondered what would happen if we made the numbers stand for something else, like for instance, the letters of the alphabet. Bingo!...We realized that we had been myopically shortsighted to think that this thing was

just an adding machine. It was something far more
exciting. It was a typewriter!"
Douglas Adams

The point Adams was making is that we should not assume that the best use of a tool is the one intended by its developers. The cell phone is an excellent example of that principle. Around the year 2000, the cell phone was used to make telephone calls, but its uses expanded very quickly until it became a multi-media communications portal. The reason this expansion succeeded is that the developers realized that the devices must be relatively simple to use. The process by which ease of use is accomplished involves inserting sophisticated software and hardware systems into the device, the details of which the user need not understand.

> "Why are video games so much better designed than office software? Because people who design video games *love to play video games*. People who design office software look forward to doing something else on the weekend."

I do not remember where I found this statement so I cannot give the author credit. But you should remember it whenever you have problems with some aspect of a technology you are using.

A columnist for the *New York Times* (Verlyn Klinkenborg) who teaches English at a college in California acquired a Blackberry in 2007 and, in response to an e-mail question from a student, sent her a text message. She told him later that she was surprised to get the message because she did not know anyone his age who sent text messages.

The admissions department of Indiana University has put all of the forms needed to enroll online. They have received complaints from some high school seniors about this, who said that "email is for old people."

Someone from the Pew Research Institute discussed a survey on text messages on National Public Radio (in December, 2009), saying that most of the billions of such messages are sent by adolescents who find the medium liberating. Even calling someone on a cell phone is too confining to them because one has to wait to see if the recipient is available

The comments Douglas Adams made about computers ended with a discussion of the Internet. He noted that at the time (1999), most sites on the world-wide-web were little more than brochures which told you what someone was selling. He contrasted that with the site used by "Amazon," which not only let you buy things directly, but let you inform the company about things you would like to buy. So the user had some input. It was the beginning of converting the web to a truly interactive medium.

Now consider educational web sites. Most are little more than brochures. They convey information but do not allow students to interact with it. An exception would be virtual reality scenarios, of which there are not too many (most of the good ones are video games), but which allow students to experience a field trip, or interactive demonstrations, etc., with varying degrees of realism. I once saw a demonstration of one that seemed quite realistic. It allowed students to make decisions about what to study, and it let them collect and analyze data. I did not actually use it myself, so I do not know if it really was as good as it seemed, but this approach to using technology is worth considering because it allows student-generated questions, which is the beginning of any useful educational exercise.

Of course, developing a Virtual Reality scenario is a time-consuming task that requires expertise in a number of disciplines, extensive technical support, and an impressive budget. That is why most educational web sites are basically brochures.

> "Computers are useless because they only give you answers."
> **Statement attributed to Pablo Picasso**

If indeed he said such a thing, Picasso was not quite correct. It is true that the computer does not teach one how to think, in that it does not teach reasoning skills that allow you to ask questions. But neither do the artist's brushes, paints, and canvas. They do not provide the questions that interest the artist either. But they, and the computer, do provide a medium *in which* one can ask questions.

The ability to ask questions does not come from knowing how to use a computer or a paintbrush. It comes from being immersed in a culture that emphasizes the importance of asking new questions. If you ask the right questions, the computer will assist in finding answers, just as oils or potting clay provide a way for an artist to examine a subject. Having the tools does not make one a scientist or an artist. Knowing what to do with them does.

In 1976 I purchased a hand-held calculator for about $80.00. Prior to that time, most calculators were much more expensive, bulky "desk-top" machines. I bought the calculator because in addition to basic arithmetic operations, it allowed me to do statistical calculations. Correlation and linear regression analyses were hard-wired into its circuits, so instead of typing data onto punch cards and taking them and a FORTRAN program, also on punch cards, to the computer center, and then waiting a day for the output, I could analyze small data sets myself at my desk. For the first time, I could ask questions of a data set easily. My productivity increased enormously thanks to this simple device. The point is that without a question in hand, there is no need for the technology. If I had been working only with large data sets the calculator would not have been useful to me. But analyzing small data sets let me develop models that could later be tested with large data sets on mainframe computers.

Asking questions about how the world works involves a way of thinking - one must set up an algorithm, which is the logical structure of the problem being studied. The computer evaluates the algorithm for a scientist. An algorithm Picasso used was the "Cubist" style with which he portrayed the world. The canvas displayed two-dimensional blocky objects to his audience. By distorting reality he forced the viewer to look for new relationships between things. To do this kind of work one must think (at least implicitly) in terms of an algorithm. Until you do that you cannot do anything useful, regardless of the technologies available to you. So, in one sense Picasso was correct - by itself, the technology is not sufficient. But he did not ask the kinds of questions that computers could answer.

Neil Postman (1999) noted that a new technology does not add or subtract things: it changes everything. He gives the example of television, which did not replace radio, it changed American culture.

Consider the large-enrollment lecture course as a technology. This approach to teaching has had more of a effect on education than any of the electronic "gadget-oriented" technologies such as Power Point, the Internet, cable television, etc. Putting several hundred students in a room for a lecture, instead of the standard classroom sizes of a dozen or two, changed the way we think about teaching introductory courses. Presenting material to two hundred people in a room is very efficient, but you are not teaching them the way you are in a small group in a small room because you cannot easily interact with them.

You cannot teach to two hundred students the way you teach to twenty, and you should not teach to twenty the way you teach to two hundred.

About all you can do in a large class is present material to be assimilated. And unfortunately, due to the size of the group, the only way you can monitor the success or failure of the communication is with the impersonal technology we call the standardized test.

We should not consider electronic technologies as competitors to the traditional approaches to teaching, but in terms of their ability to change the way we think about teaching. Such changes are bound to happen, but will they be beneficial to the students? To convert an *in-a-classroom* large-enrollment course into an *on-line* large-enrollment course does not seem to provide many benefits to the students. Even the asynchronous nature of an on-line course, which allows students to work on material when they choose, instead of requiring them to be in a room at a specific time, is not too significant a change if the material is covered in the same manner as in the traditionally taught classes. As I contended earlier, a one-to-one mapping of the traditional course into an on-line course changes how the teaching is done, but has little effect on the learning.

In principle, teaching and learning should be improved by the use of new technologies. In practice, it is difficult to demonstrate improvement because few teachers have the luxury of using control groups to determine the effects of changes they make in their teaching. So the majority of the evidence for improved teaching or learning due to the use of various technologies seems to be anecdotal.

When someone claims that listening to audio or video tapes of lectures is equivalent to being present at a lecture, I have to wonder how good the lecture was. Recorded lectures are based on the assumption that teaching is equivalent to telling students things. Consider the videotapes of the Psychology lectures I mentioned in Chapter 1. They were well done, in that the presentations were smooth, but they were examples of one-way communication. The students could not ask questions and the instructor had no way to know if the students understood what was said during the presentation. A "canned" lecture cannot be equivalent to the original. Only those who do not appreciate the spontaneity of (at least some) classroom presentations can believe that a recorded presentation is adequate.

> "Most of us know by this time that when we are told that the pattern of something has been much improved, it means that all of its distinctive characteristics have disappeared."
> **G. K. Chesterton (1927)**

It seems clear that with respect to computers, the machine itself is not important; after all, it is just a fancy adding machine. The important technology is the software, because software changes the way we think about things. The first spreadsheet, Visicalc, prompted the PC revolution because people realized that the program was useful in a variety of ways. Regardless of how powerful desktop computers are today, the utility is still in the software. Any software package that allows us to do things has the potential to affect society. I can ask questions using it. I do not have to be a professional programmer to solve time-consuming problems when I have access to a spreadsheet because the program does the heavy lifting, just as the statistical package hard-wired into my calculator made me more productive in the 1970s.

Educational technologies that merely present information to students are neither revolutionary nor interesting. On the other hand, technologies that work by enabling students to do new things are both interesting, and sometimes even revolutionary.

It may not be easy to determine what advantages new technologies provide an instructor. If you now use existing technologies that work, why change? Will a new technology allow you to do something you think important but cannot do now? Is the new application important enough to make changing your existing approach worth the effort and cost? Are new things always better than old things? Or are the claims made by those who must have every innovation merely a modern example of the process that Herbert Butterfield called "Whig History?"

There are many aspects to the new electronic technologies and a number of them involve images. Students like to see movies in class, partly because they represent a change from the oral lecture, and perhaps partly because they think they understand the point of films more easily than lectures. Everyone watches images on television, so everyone thinks they are experts at interpreting visual images. Unfortunately, people tend to forget that images are iconic in nature, and cannot be interpreted the way that information presented using a serial medium such as a conversation or a lecture can be. People tend to think that words must be understood but images are self-explanatory.

Even when a sound track is present, students tend to concentrate on the images in a film. I did an experiment once on this matter. While I showed a film, I had students take notes on sheets of paper that I collected afterward, so I could determine what impressed them the most. I thought that because the actor Ted Danson narrated the film the students would be attentive, but I was wrong. The notes showed that the majority of students in the class largely ignored the sound track, but they were strongly influenced by the visual images. In a section on the pollution of Puget Sound, most of the students took notes about the images shown of the diseased liver of a fish caught in the bay, but no one's notes referred to the cause of the disease, the heavily industrialized nature of the area surrounding the bay, even though that was mentioned several times in the sound track. Similar things showed up in their notes concerning other parts of the film.

The visual "punches" impressed them much more than the words that were telling the story. It seems clear to me that technologies that involve extensive use of images require much more careful thought than those that rely on written messages.

> "The compass, gunpowder, and printing have changed the course of the world. Yet it never occurred to the Chinese, who discovered them, that they had in their hands the means of endlessly disturbing the earth's repose. To us, this is scandalous."
> **Paul Valery**

In other words, if it can be done, it should be done. If you have a technology, you must use it. Valery also said: "Nothing...is harder for us to imagine than putting a limit on the mind's will and using material power with moderation." These comments were made in 1895 but the ideas behind them are still pertinent to western society and its educational system.

> When you use a hammer to drive a nail you are using a tool. When you throw a switch to turn on a machine you are using a technology, one with an elaborate network that supports your efforts.

In the early 1960s, living in Boston, I knew a woman who was at least 75 years old at the time. She told me once about trips she and her late husband made to visit relatives in New Jersey, *circa* WWI. Today, the drive would take four to five hours on the interstate highway system. At that time it took a few days because there were no paved roads (much less highways), no road maps, and no gas stations in every small village. A trip across three or four states was an expedition. The automobile the couple used was a tool but they could not call upon any more support for their trip than those traveling by horseback could.

The support systems we use today allow us to make trips like that in much less time, and in much more comfort. We need not wear dusters and goggles, the roads are smoother, the suspensions in modern automobiles provide a much more comfortable ride, and facilities are available at regular intervals. Without that level of support, we might as well use horses to take trips. In fact, without paved roads, most cars would be less effective than a horse.

As technologies develop, continued access depends on continued development of the support systems. Our choices are not always as effective as we would like to think; if we are too quick to buy the latest technology we may not be able to use it. Because I live in a rural area, I wrote the first draft of these words on a computer connected to the Internet by a 56k modem which usually connected at about 45k. The computer I used had an adequate memory for most tasks, so in principle I could view the image files friends sent to me on occasion. But the time involved in downloading the images was more than I was willing to spend, so I routinely asked people not to send me messages that contained the latest pictures of their cat or dog doing something cute. Someone once said:

A picture may be worth a thousand words, but do you know how many megabytes it requires?

The limitations imposed by the Internet connection represent a bottleneck that negates the advantages a modern computer provides. The telephone company finally provided DSL service to the house, so now I have no excuse to avoid looking at pictures of my friends' pets.

Technology is not a machine. Machines need a social organization to become technologies. Instead, technology is a value system that supports some of our activities. For example, the cell phone allows us to do a variety of things we could not do on the landline telephones. Of course, some of us who grew up using a telephone only to make and receive calls do not use the new phones effectively. I personally do not feel the need to send text messages or to access the Internet while driving or walking. And I have never felt the need to take a picture and send it immediately to a friend. So the cell phone I usually carry (in my car, not in my pocket) may do more than make and receive calls (I am not actually sure) but I do not use it for anything else.

But the ubiquity of cell phones, and the fact that most people value the ability to do many things with a phone wherever they happen to be, has resulted in some significant changes in our society. In the past, when people made calls from telephone booths, the conversations were private. Nearly everyone closed the door to the booth so no one could eavesdrop, and someone waiting to use the phone usually stood a few feet back from the booth to avoid appearing to eavesdrop. Today, no one seems to mind being overheard, because people make and receive calls in public settings in the most casual manner. In some venues (concert halls and hospitals) the management asks people to turn off their phones so they will not be disruptive. A recent (2009) review of a Broadway play noted that when a cell phone rang in the hall, the principal actor turned to the audience and asked the fellow with the phone to answer it so he could go on with his part. The message I get from some of the changes caused by this technology is that rude behavior is the norm today.

Recall Neil Postman's comment that a new technology has the potential to effect significant societal changes.

Another example. While sitting in the office of the dean of a graduate school, sometime in the 1990s, waiting for a meeting to begin, I noticed that the receptionist never answered the telephone. Instead, she continued typing and let the answering machine take the calls. Presumably, someone dealt with all of the calls at once, after regular office hours. I commented to the dean that her office was very important to the community because it was the gateway for people who wanted to enroll in one or two courses as non-degree students (I heard of a retired Dentist who enrolled in an art course every semester). But the response prospective students received when they called told them that they were not important enough to speak to a live person. The reason for this approach to dealing with the public was, of course, economic; the dean's budget would not allow her to hire an extra person to answer the telephone.

Today, I hardly ever get a live person when I call some large organization. I nearly always have to work my way down several levels of an automated response system that has the structure of a tree diagram. Sometimes I have to call several times to make sure the system directs me to the correct "branch" of the tree. When I make such calls I usually hear a recording saying that "my call is very important to them," whereas, clearly, my time is not.

> To "...paraphrase the philosopher Wittgenstein, a medium of communication may be a vehicle of thought but we must not forget that it is also the driver."
> **Neil Postman (1988)**

Now think about how we teach introductory courses in college classrooms. The message sent by the way we teach these courses is that the purpose of a college or university is to accept large numbers of students and give them degrees in the most efficient way, not necessarily to educate them. If someone manages to get an education, everyone is pleased; the deans congratulate themselves; but the purpose of the system is to process large numbers of people. So, like the social setting created by cell phones and answering machines, the one involved with large lecture courses is also normative. It is not value-neutral because it sends messages about what school is for. Students understand these messages, which is probably one reason they have so little respect for the trappings of the university; many of them realize that they are considered to be little more than cash-cows whose money allows the system to do what it considers more important than providing educations for its customers.

We hear and read about how an information-based society is emerging - that information is no longer a fixed commodity, stored in a repository called a school, to be doled out carefully to a select few. We hear that the proliferation of computers and the development of resources such as the Internet will decentralize knowledge - will turn people from recipients to manipulators. Of course, claims such as these are not new: Ivan Illich called for decentralizing the educational system long before the development of electronic technologies.

But can our educational system change itself? The university as an institution is dedicated to doing things largely as they were done in the past. For example, cap and gown ceremonies are a relic of the medieval university, and the average university curriculum concentrates on tradition. The parochial high school at which I taught in the 1970s required students to wear uniforms, mainly to reassure parents that the school had not changed significantly from the time that they attended it. The pressure to change the way we think about teaching has always come largely from outside the educational institutions, not from within. Students cannot see how their education prepares them for the world they will enter, and most of them realize that their career tracks will not involve academic research.

Speaking of college professors, O'Donnell said:

> "If we think we are in the information business, we make the...mistake of confusing a tool with a goal. The real strength of the professor has always been as an organizer, an evaluator, and a processor."

Few if any of your students care about the research you do but many could benefit from learning about the thought processes you use in doing the work. The information-based society provides many opportunities for instructors to teach about data collection and analysis. You do not have to be a librarian to understand how information is categorized. You do not have to be a mathematician to know how to use software to sort through a data set to find something relevant to your community. But you *do* have to recognize what kinds of opportunities exist and how to exploit them. "Meta-cognition" is more than a bit of jargon used by Psychologists: it identifies ways of thinking that everyone should use.

Shoshanna Zuboff provided three case studies that addressed the question of whether computers cause people to think differently. Her results indicate that a technology such as the computer *can* change the way people on a job think, but such changes are not inevitable because they depend on the organizational structure of the industry involved.

Her first example was the paper industry. The introduction of computer control systems changed the infrastructure in a plant that converted pulp into paper. The new system had computers monitoring the processes in the plant that allowed the workers to ask questions about activities that were not possible before. And it was *necessary* for them to ask the questions in order to deal with problems that developed. For example, if the viscosity of the product at some point was not correct, the workers could ask for temperature data "upstream" from that point. But they had to know what questions to ask and for what stage in the process to ask them. So they had to develop a mental model of the entire plant. With such a model they could ask relevant questions and formulate decisions about the cause of a problem and how to deal with it. Then they could issue electronic orders to implement the decisions. Prior to the implementation of the new system, workers sensing a problem in production could only walk around and bang the pipes with a wrench to get things working again.

Zuboff emphasized that the information used to develop the mental models was available because management was willing to let line workers have access to it. It was not available to them before the introduction of the automated control system because there was no way for them to use it in the past.

In a real estate office application, the results were different. The computers were given to clerks who used them as word processors. The structure of decision-making did not change, so no cognitive changes were observed in how the clerks did their job. The third example involved a bank in South America, in which the results were equivocal.

Zuboff's results indicate that although it is important to ask what a technology *can* do, it is just as important to ask *what it will be allowed* to do.

Much of the material in this book was retrieved from a journal I kept for a number of years, writing items in spiral bound notebooks. Eventually I shifted to using a word processor and stored comments in electronic files. Some of the material that might have been included in this book was lost when my computer's hard drive crashed. That provides a warning to be diligent about maintaining backups of computer files, because modern technologies in the form of electronic media do not provide the kind of permanency that paper notebooks do. A book printed in The 16th Century can easily be read today. A file stored on one of the original "floppy" discs in the 1980s cannot be retrieved.

EPILOGUE

What kinds of skills do we think students should have? Perhaps the ability to:

Recognize the existence of a problem;

Learn how to simplify a problem so it can be solved;

Identify what is needed to solve the problem;

Recognize whether the solution can be used in some way.

Pick a technology and ask how its use will enable students to attain these skills. If it is not obvious how it will enable your students to do such things, then that technology has not made you irrelevant.

DISTANCE EDUCATION

"...(Filmmakers changed) a mere recording technology
into an expressive medium."
Janet Murray

Murray pointed out that in the first few decades of the 20th
Century filmmakers created a medium by inventing the elements
of telling stories on film - the car chase, the close-up, etc. She
says that they did all this by studying the "properties" of film:
the effects of moving the camera, adjusting the lens aperture, the
focus, etc.

Can we say analogous things about the proponents of distance
education? Have they been experimenting with techniques within
each of the media to develop new ways for students to learn?
Or have they just been transferring classes from one medium to
another? The proliferation of lecture courses on DVD that I see
advertised in magazines suggests that much of what is being done
involves little more than simple transfers.

In an ideal situation, converting an existing course to a distance education format would be analogous to transforming a doughnut into a coffee cup. Mathematicians tell us that the two items are equivalent because one can be changed to the other smoothly, in that no new holes or surfaces need be created. One edge of the doughnut can be squeezed down to form the depression that holds the coffee and the hole in the doughnut becomes the cup handle. A simple, elegant transformation. But regardless of what the technical people would have us believe, in practice, the mapping of courses from one medium to another is not smooth, simple or elegant.

The traditional lecture is a quasi-structured presentation. There are long-term goals and specific objectives, but the manner in which they are reached vary, as the instructor feels the need. The time spent on some aspect of the subject, the associations made, even the order in which the material is covered may vary with the audience and the mood of the instructor. The distance education instructor does not often have that flexibility.

I have grumbled for many years about the defects of large-enrollment lecture courses. I taught them for more than 20 years, at least twice and, counting summer sessions, sometimes four times a year. I think I did a good job presenting the material, in that I was able to explain complex topics clearly. But although I knew how the students did on standardized tests, I did not know how much they actually learned about the subjects, because the format did not allow me to go much beyond multiple-choice tests for evaluation.

An ego-deflating event occurred to me once when a woman came up to me in a campus snack bar and said she had taken one of my lecture courses a few years before. She went on to say that she remembered me and my course because I was one of the two instructors she remembered who spoke English correctly, consistently. I thanked her for the compliment, though I am sure that my speech patterns are not as good as she claimed. Whose are? But I wondered to myself why that was the only thing she remembered about the course. Was there not something about the content that she remembered? I decided not to ask her that, for fear of getting an honest answer.

Though the atmosphere in a large lecture hall is not conducive to small group discussions, these classes are not necessarily soporific because the "shape" of a lecture is a bit nebulous. It is largely oral, but as mentioned above, it is only partly structured. Like Homer and other epic poets, who told largely the same stories over and over again, but who tailored them to the audience sitting around a campfire, and who sometimes added flourishes (if they perhaps had had an extra cup of wine that evening), experienced lecturers usually sense when students do not understand something, or are bored by the material, and adapt their presentation spontaneously to accommodate the audience. The overall teaching objectives can still be met, even when time is spent repeating material or on anecdotes that change the pace a bit.

Finding effective distance education alternatives to this kind of spontaneity is not straightforward, and is not even possible in some formats.

> "Are we going to be working for a smart machine, or
> will we have smart people around the machine?"
> **Shoshanna Zuboff**

The quote comes from the book by Zuboff, but it is said by an anonymous plant manager. Zuboff goes on to say that"

> "Building the smart machine preserves the boundaries
> between those who command and those who obey.
> Surrounding the machine with smart people can
> undermine those boundaries and introduce a new
> ambiguity into the rationale for managerial authority."

If all you have is money you might as well build the smart machine. In the educational context that means adding every new technological feature as it is developed. That choice cements relationships by establishing who is making the important pedagogical decisions. But if you have smart people, you can be more selective about what to use. You can let smart instructors decide what is appropriate for what they want to do. At another level, you can let smart students follow their own paths (*cf.* Ryle's comments in Chapter 1 on writing sonnets). That relegates the technical experts to the background, where they belong in an academic environment. If you wish to change the way your students learn material, you will not be successful if you follow the paths indicated by those who designed the infrastructure.

Freeman Dyson discussed two ways technologies can develop. One way involves government oversight and funding, and the other involves small-scale innovations by entrepreneurs. He noted the activities between the two world wars to design airplanes. Many small companies were founded, based on a variety of designs. Some of these companies failed because of poor design and others because of poor implementation. Those which survived did so because their designs and business models were adequate to the tasks. He pointed out that if a government agency had decided to fund the development of an aircraft industry, little innovation would have occurred and the resulting design probably would not have been as effective as those of the entrepreneurs. Eventually, a few large corporations developed that swallowed up the small companies, but that is another story.

With respect to educational technology, top-down oversight will produce some tools that will be used to teach students, but funding decisions made by administrators will prevent many ideas that could be worthwhile from developing. The results of bottom-up decision making will look messy at first, but the "let a thousand flowers bloom" philosophy has the potential to produce approaches that work.

The original example of distance education is the traditional correspondence course. Students who register for such a course are issued a textbook and a study guide. The guide is designed to "talk them through" the textbook, and to add material considered important which is not covered in the book.

In each section of the study guide the students are provided with points to consider when reading the book, and with some questions to answer (along with the answers) to provide some immediate feedback on how well they understand the material. Then they answer another set of questions and mail them to the person monitoring their progress (the "instructor"). When they finish a specified number of chapters, the students go to a learning center where they take a supervised test. At the end of the course they take the final examination, again, at a learning center. All this is usually required to occur within a one-year time frame.

Instead of the term "distance" education, this approach to learning about a topic might just as easily be called "individualized" education," because the students communicate with their "instructor" only by U.S. mail or by telephone, and they never meet with others who might be taking the course. It is a totally impersonal approach to teaching and learning.

Now consider the traditional large-enrollment lecture course. Students go to a large classroom twice a week and listen to the instructor talk about the subject. Some (but not all) instructors encourage questions from the students, and some (but not all) attempt to involve the students by asking questions of them, or by having them work through examples during the class. A variety of audio-visual aids may be used (slides, films, the Internet, etc.) but the teaching style for the most part involves talking. Students are encouraged to take notes, sometimes they are given assignments to turn in, and once or twice a semester they take a standardized test in addition to the final examination, another standardized test.

Anyone who has taught one of these courses realizes that the large room results in an impersonal atmosphere. It provides a place for students who wish to be anonymous to sit in the back of the room where they can feel "safe." The ones in the back usually do not wish to be called upon and usually do not ask questions. They do not wish to participate. They are doing the equivalent of "lurking" on a listserv in an on-line course. And as the semester proceeds, fewer and fewer of them come to class.

If one considers only the atmosphere in the classroom, there is a striking similarity between the impersonal nature of the large-enrollment lecture course and that of a correspondence course. It does not matter if students actually come to a room and listen to a lecture if they sit in the back so they can be "removed" from the intellectual activities going on up front. A substantial number of students in these lecture courses might as well be taking a correspondence course. In fact, the correspondence course requires more of them than most lecture courses because students are required to turn in assignments on a regular schedule.

"social systems...express relationships of authority that reflect a particular distribution of power and...of opportunity."
Shoshanna Zuboff

She goes on to say that one's development is strongly affected by the opportunities to learn and practice what one learns. Unless role requirements and social conditions are flexible, growth opportunities are limited.

The undergraduate educational system is really not set up to foster inquiry; it is designed for the presentation of content. Curious students may not feel comfortable raising points in a class because some instructors clearly feel that they must cover a specific amount of material, and show some annoyance when interrupted by questions. Even when questions are encouraged, quite often the response to a question is an answer, not an invitation to look into the matter.

> The Medium is *not* the Message.
> The *Method* is the Message.

Pace, Marshall McLuhan. This comment is something to remember anytime you consider changing the format of a course from the traditional lecture model to some form of distance education. It does not matter which medium you choose; what you *do* with it is what is important.

> "You cannot dismantle the master's house with the master's tools."
> **Audre Lord**

This comment is a subtle way to suggest that power relationships should be considered when making changes. In another context, W. Edwards Deming noted that stable systems are very stable, in that incremental changes do not produce noticeable effects on their performance; substantial structural changes are required to have an effect. So how can we change the educational system?

Some distance education approaches show promise in this regard because they require more of the students than canned answers to canned questions. The on-line course is the most obvious way to let students break out of the traditional passive learning component of the system. The asynchronous format, and the fact that contact with an instructor is minimized in such courses, put the burden on the students, so opportunities for intellectual growth are increased.

At this point I should distinguish between merely converting an introductory lecture course to an on-line course, and creating a new on-line course dealing with material on an introductory level. Converting from one format to another is not easy because you have to think about the structure of the existing course, not just the content.

It is very important for the instructor making such a change to make clear distinctions between goals, skills, and strategies.

> The goals are things you want students to know after the unit is completed.

> The learning skills are things students must be able to do in order to achieve the goals.

> The teaching strategies are things the instructor must do to make sure students have the skills needed to achieve the goals.

This three-way breakdown is appropriate for any class on any subject, but it is very important in planning distance education courses because the strategies will vary considerably from those used in a traditional classroom setting.

Note that the students will be tested on how well they achieve the goals, so it is important that the teaching strategies address the learning skills, not the goals. If the strategies address the goals, you will be "teaching to the test." This is why the distinction between the three components shown in the table below, which represents the structure of a class on the size of an earthquake, is important.

Goals	Necessary Learning Skills	Teaching Strategies
Understand Magnitude and Intensity and distinguish between them.	Must be able to decipher scientific text.	Give them practice in finding the "patterns" in scientific text.
Understand how Magnitude is determined.	Be able to use the nomogram in the handout that takes data and gives Magnitude	Explain that the nomogram solves an equation, and give practice in its use.
Understand how Intensity is determined.	Must be able to see patterns in damage reports	Give them practice in ranking types of damage.

Understand how Intensity is used.	Must understand relationship between damage and ground velocity	Have them read about the shaking of a building and how it affects structural stability.

This approach to teaching makes sense because it concentrates on having the students do most of the heavy lifting (*i.e.* developing the learning skills). Given the right resources they should be able to infer much of what I would want them to learn from a lecture on the topic. And, in addition to content (the goals), they should learn something about how one learns about a topic (a meta skill) by collecting information and analyzing it.

But I was wary of using this approach in a traditional classroom setting. I could easily deliver a lecture on the size of an earthquake and the damage done by it in one class period, but working through each of the teaching strategies given in the table would require a lot of class time. Covering the material in this manner would force me to jettison other topics in the course to make room for the hands-on exercises. So any time I did some experiments aimed at changing the atmosphere in my lecture courses, I had to make some hard decisions about what to jettison.

Note my reluctance to emphasize learning over teaching.

On the other hand, the asynchronous nature of an on-line course is ideally suited to this approach because students can work at their own pace at times chosen by them.

The choice is simple: do you want to teach the material or do you want your students to learn the material?

The components of the table above are appropriate for any distance education course but the teaching strategies will vary, depending on the format of the medium used. That is an important point because:

The medium will dictate the strategies that are appropriate and the strategies will determine to a large extent what the students will learn.

So the strategies will have to be compatible with the medium. For example, the strategies in the table above would not work in a course taught on cable television because "canned" lectures emphasize teaching rather than learning. They represent only a small change from the traditional large-enrollment lecture course. Courses taught using interactive television might utilize this approach effectively, but they would require that a supervisor familiar with the material be present at each location.

An important question that anyone who wants to teach an on-line course should consider is:

> If you are not going to lecture, what are you going to do?

In other words, what value are you going to provide the students? Why are you needed in a distance education course, in which you are not personally "teaching" the students? After all, they have a textbook for the content, so why do they need you? If you cannot answer that question, perhaps you should think more about the difference between teaching and learning.

The asynchronous nature of the on-line format provides the flexibility that allows students to get hands-on experience which is not easily done in traditionally-taught introductory courses in large lecture halls. With the use of a listserv for communications between students and between students and the instructor, fruitful interactions between beginners are possible as they work through the tasks called for by the teaching strategies. This is one approach to dealing with the problems associated with the large-enrollment lecture courses that are supposed to introduce students to a discipline, but which merely give them practice in taking and memorizing notes for the next test. With the right approach, you can give them ways to internalize the material that is not possible in the traditional lecture format.

At different times I was exposed to a few of the technologies used in distance education. I took part in some meetings using interactive television, and once a lecture of mine on earthquakes in the Midwest was videotaped for a colleague's cable television course (My presentation was adequate, but not nearly as smooth as those on the tapes created for the Psychology course mentioned in Chapter 1). But my main experience in distance education involved the creation and teaching of an on-line course which I taught for about eight semesters, before retiring from teaching. What follows is a description of the course, because it illustrates by how much my approach to teaching was changed by that experience.

For most of my career, I taught introductory courses as everyone else did, by lecturing. But I did not "teach" in the on-line course as much as I monitored students' learning. The tools used in the course consisted of a listserv and two web sites. The listserv provided a way for students to communicate with each other and with me. It also allowed me to monitor the discussions between students, which allowed me to keep track of which students were working and which were not. One of the web sites contained material I posted to introduce students to the topic to be covered and the other allowed them to post some of the material they were developing, so everyone in their group could use it.

The class size was usually between 40 and 50 students, but one semester 75 were enrolled. To keep track of who was doing what, I divided the class into groups of about 20 to 25 students each. The separating was done alphabetically by name because I felt that that was the simplest way to get a random selection of students in each group.

The students completed three projects in a semester, each of which involved writing a paper on a topic. Each time they went through four steps:

- they developed an outline for the paper;

- they refined the outline, working with other students on the listserv;

- they searched the Internet for references on the topics in the outline;

- they wrote the paper.

The most important part of the course involved having the students decide what to study. At the beginning of each project I informed them that they were to write a five-page paper on a topic such as global warming, so the first thing they had to do was to create an outline of what should be in such a paper, and send it to the listserv. General background material was available on one of the web sites so everyone could start the project at about the same level of knowledge.

After about a week, I suggested that they look at all of the outlines that were posted by members of their group to see if items in other students' outlines might improve their own. If so, they should modify theirs and post a new outline. Once this had been done a couple of times, many of the outlines resembled each other, so I posted several on the listserv and asked the students to "vote on" the one they liked the best. The one which received the most votes was the one they were going to use to write their papers.

When the voting ended, I took the most favored outline and posted it on an interactive web site. On this site, each topic in the outline became a live link to a message form to which students could post material. I told them to go to the Internet and find articles relevant to each item on the outline. They were to summarize the articles and post them in the appropriate places on the web site. No one had to find articles for all of the items; each student's grade for that component of the project depended more on the quality of the summaries than on their number.

After a week or two, the web site contained several summaries for each item in the outline. The result was an annotated bibliography for the topic, to which every student had access. Then I told them to write their papers, using that outline and those references. While I graded the papers (submitted to me on paper), I had them start on the next project, using the same approach.

It was interesting to see how different groups developed different outlines for a given topic. Each student decided what was appropriate for the topic and then, by interacting with others in the group, modified his/her outline to come up with a final version. So they had to work by themselves and then collaborate with others. I did not intervene in the process unless I thought a group was including material in its outline for which there were too few resources on the Internet.

Many instructors are not comfortable with assigning group projects because they cannot be sure who is working and who is not; we all know that some students tend to coast, letting others do most of the work. In my course, by monitoring the "traffic" on the listserv, I knew exactly who was working and who was not. With this information I could assign grades based on who submitted outlines (and how complete they were), on who participated in improving the outlines, on who posted decent summaries of reference materials for the bibliography, as well as who could write a decent paper once all of the materials were in hand. Their grades reflected the extent of their participation in the project as well as the quality of their writing.

At regular intervals, I pointed out to the students that the hardest part of writing a paper involved deciding what should be in it. Most students add material as they find resources in the library, resulting in papers that are not structured well. So creating the outline was an important first step. Once it was developed, the rest was easy because the outline focused their attention on which articles they found on the Internet were relevant and which ones could be ignored.

I also pointed out that this sequence of steps (developing an outline, the search for references, writing of the paper) *could be used in any course they might take*. It was an example of a technique that was transferable to any discipline, and it would save them time when writing papers on any topic in any course.

The students who took this course did not necessarily learn what I would have discussed in a traditional lecture course, but that did not bother me (Recall the woman who remembered only my speech patterns in one of my lecture courses). But the students did learn some things about each topic discussed, and by doing the work themselves, they learned how to learn about a subject. So I considered the course a success.

Just because a course is asynchronous does not mean that it has to be "distant."

The on-line format has the potential to be as "distant" as a correspondence course, but I found that students in the one I taught were not intimidated by its asynchronous nature. I have had as many as 75 students working effectively (in three separate groups). In addition to course-related materials, students used the listserv to send a variety of kinds of messages to each other. For example, when one student announced that he was getting engaged he was advised to let his fiancé handle all of the wedding preparations; another student said she would be gone during

Spring Break on her honeymoon; someone else asked the group where she could find a recycling center, and received a response; and another apologized for what someone else took to be personal criticism. In short, some semblance of a community developed over the course of each semester, even though most of the students did not know and never saw each other, or me. That never seemed to happen in the large-enrollment lecture courses I taught for many years.

For a variety of reasons, it is more difficult to teach on-line courses than the traditional ones. One problem is psychological. To use the on-line format effectively, instructors have to get over the belief that their physical presence is required for learning to occur. You need to set up the exercises properly, turn the students loose, and see what happens. Do not assume that you are the dispenser of all important knowledge; let the traditional roles of teacher and student become fluid. As long as you keep track of what the students are doing you can monitor the learning that is occurring, something that the chair of your department needs to be reassured about.

Another reason involves time. I spent many hours each day monitoring the listserv to keep track of what was happening. When I retired, the logical people to take on the course were reluctant to do it because they were too busy publishing papers and writing grant proposals in order to get tenure. That was discouraging but understandable, considering how the educational system works today. So I decided to think of the course as one of the "thousand flowers" that bloomed at that time. At any given time other flowers are blooming and will be as effective as I feel that mine was.

EPILOGUE

G. K. Chesterton (1904) began one of his novels by saying that the public treats prophets politely, listening to what they say and applauding at the right times. Then, as soon as the prophet dies, the public does the opposite of what was prophesied. But Chesterton was not aware of how quickly situations can change. Those of us who write on a subject such as distance education should be aware that our comments may become obsolete well within our own lifetimes.

Nevertheless, as I read articles on how various technologies are used to expand teaching beyond the traditional classroom I wonder how many of the innovative approaches described in the articles will survive the instructors. When someone retires, will another faculty member be willing to pick up his or her course? Or must students wait for someone else (who has tenure) to devise another innovative approach to the use of some technology in teaching? It seems clear that if technology were a panacea for the teaching profession innovations would be cumulative and it would not be necessary for everyone to re-invent the wheel.

SCIENTIFIC LITERACY

> "If a man burns to learn and sets himself to comparing
> his ideas with experimental results in order that he
> may correct those ideas, every scientific man will
> recognize him as a brother no matter how small his
> knowledge may be."
> **Charles Sanders Peirce**

What does it mean to be scientifically literate? I know of no simple definition that would satisfy very many people, but Peirce's statement provides a way to start constructing a definition. Intellectual activity is the key, he feels. Who would disagree with that? To go further, let's consider something Alfred North Whitehead said in a broader context.

> "Culture is activity of thought. Receptiveness to beauty
> and humane feelings. Facts have nothing to do with it.
> The merely well-informed man is the most useless bore
> on God's earth."

There is enough in the two quotations to cobble something together. Self-correcting activities. Receptiveness. Activity of thought. Facts are immaterial. These are useful building blocks. One must be receptive to new ideas and capable of analyzing or interpreting them, and one must be willing to discard old ideas when appropriate. It matters little how much you know; what is important is what you do with what you know. That is a good start but it is not very specific. Activity of thought should be related to learning, so let's consider that.

Learning is an internal process that cannot easily be taught because learning to learn is a meta-skill. Aiming students in certain directions is the key. A good teacher does not merely tell students things, because:

> "Once known, truths acquire a utilitarian crust; they no longer interest us as truths but as useful recipes."
> **Jose Ortega y Gassett**

Ortega goes on to say that "He who wishes to teach us a truth should place us in a position to discover it ourselves." Discovery provides more associations with previous knowledge than does that which is told to us in classrooms. Remember your own classroom experiences? You probably were too busy taking notes to consciously think about associations, so what was told to you went into your notes, not necessarily into your mind. It is not easy to become proficient in a subject if you are restricted to taking notes and trying to figure out what they mean later.

Of course, learning is not confined to what goes on in academic environments. In fact, one could argue that relatively little learning occurs in classrooms because of the need to take a good set of notes. But many people in our society, who have no academic credentials routinely satisfy Peirce's condition. Orchid breeders, cat and dog breeders, and chefs are examples of people who experiment within their specialties to "push the envelope" a bit. They "fool around," hoping to produce something better or new.

In principle, their activities should have been affected by the money spent by the National Science Foundation for the last 50 or so years to improve the level of science education in the public schools and college and universities. I write *should have* because it is not clear how to relate the activities of a local garden club or kennel club to a particular school curriculum. Perhaps an improved high school science class gave some of the breeders and chefs an interest in what they do now as a hobby or an occupation. Or perhaps their schooling had nothing to do with it; perhaps they developed their skills because there are more social networks, such as master gardening programs, dog and cat shows, etc., than there were in the past. Whatever the reason, a number of people are experimenting with one thing or another, and although few of them think of themselves as scientists, some of them are proceeding in a scientific manner.

This experiential approach to a definition should produce people who satisfy Peirce's criterion, so some reasonable percentage of the population may well be more scientifically literate than in the past, albeit not necessarily in ways that were intended by federal funding programs. On the other hand, although the systematic activities undertaken by some gardeners, breeders, etc., seem *necessary* to be considered scientific, are they *sufficient*? Should more be required of them for us to consider them scientifically literate?

Perhaps what they learn should be transferable to other disciplines. If the dog breeder decides to raise orchids, can he "hit the ground running?" That is, is what was learned about genetics in one discipline transferable to another? Clearly, the details are not transferable, but has the dog breeder learned enough of the general principles of genetics to move easily into another discipline? Or shift to something completely new, such as gourmet cooking? The ability to do such things would suggest a considerable degree of intellectual maturity, but would we call it "scientific" maturity? So Peirce's criterion may not be sufficient. Perhaps an adequate definition should include the ability to proceed in a scientific manner, but also include the ability to generalize from what one has learned so that a person can recognize associations (or utilize meta-associations) to other situation and disciplines. Note the word "associations." I don't seem to be able to get away from it.

Recall Roger Schank's concept of semantic memory. We learn from experience by broadening the spectrum of what kinds of things can happen, not by keeping track of everything that has happened and the order in which they happened. Broadening the spectrum would seem to be necessary to infer the general principles that allow a person to apply knowledge to new situations.

This approach to defining scientific literacy is subject to criticism because it is very general. Perhaps it is too general, in that it encompasses so many people with so many different interests that the term "scientific literacy" may make little sense. Perhaps a more traditional criterion is the only sensible one to use for a topic as important as this. A very conservative definition would probably require that one major in science in college. This much more stringent approach to a definition would reduce the size of the group considerably. And would what remains really be indicative of a scientifically literate group?

Of course, possession of a degree in science does not guarantee that a person thinks like a scientist. I know someone with a degree in science who is also a numerologist. And I met a salesman with a degree in Chemistry who believes in ghosts. And years ago I knew a Civil Engineer and a physician who were creationists.

So perhaps a broad definition of scientific literacy is not meaningless. If people are doing things systematically and finding ways to improve what they are doing, does it matter what sort of a background in science they have? Perhaps we need not go much beyond Peirce's definition.

Ever since the Soviet Union launched Sputnik in 1957, the National Science Foundation has provided enormous amounts of money to increase the number of scientists and engineers in this country, and to improve the science courses in the public schools. Curricula were developed, teacher-training programs were funded, and equipment grants were provided to science and engineering faculty. But there were so many facets to the effort that it is not clear which worked and which did not. The percentage of the population going into science and engineering may have increased, but how do we determine if the scientific literacy of the general population has improved due to these programs? By "general population," I mean those people with a high school diploma who did not attend college, as well as those who majored in some non-science discipline in college.

Anecdotal evidence is not encouraging. Regardless of the number of people in kennel and gardening clubs, there is reason to believe that members of the general population do not know much more about science than the average person did 50 years ago.

> Consider that in 2008 three candidates for the Republican nomination for the presidency stated in a debate on television that they did not believe in Evolution. A few days later, one of them had an op-ed piece in the *New York Times* that hedged his position a bit. I guess his handlers did not want him to seem too regressive. But the statements made at the debate clearly were aimed at the "religious right" segment of the Republican Party, so the implication is that a substantial number of people are sympathetic to the statements made in the debate, statements which reject the foundation of modern Biology. That is not promising.

> Consider that many newspapers have an astrology section but few have one on astronomy or on any other aspect of science.

> Consider that a large number of people believe in a literal interpretation of the Bible, including the creation stories in the *Book of Genesis*. The numbers are so large that pressure often is exerted on school districts to teach the "biblical account" along with the "scientific account" so students can decide for themselves which to believe.

> Consider that some people claim that a county government is not endorsing Christianity when it posts the Ten Commandments in the courthouse, but they feel that a Biology teacher is endorsing atheism if biblical interpretations are not included in a science class.

What do such disputes imply about the general educational level (much less the degree of scientific literacy) of the population?

Would you trust any of these people to make informed decisions on scientific matters? Would you trust them to teach your children and grandchildren? What about our elected officials, who *do* make decisions about the funding of scientific studies?

Is it possible to overcome the kinds of thinking mentioned above? The prospect is not promising. To make some sense out of the current situation it is useful to consider some ideas examined by Farhad Majoo. He suggested that the process of "selective exposure" explains why political discussions have become so polarized. The proliferation of sources of information on the Internet is so extreme that it is easy for people to avoid contact with any ideas that contradict their own. When you are exposed to a wide spectrum of ideas you have to do some work to evaluate them, and in doing so, you might be convinced to change your mind from time to time. But when the content of everything you read and hear is similar, it is easy for that material to become "cemented" in your thinking. That bias is bound to affect the way you make decisions.

Majoo then went on to discuss the consequences of selective exposure. He was interested in how people with different opinions who are exposed to the same event (say a football game) can come away with different perceptions of that material. He called the mechanism "selective perception," and said that when your opinion differs from that of the fellow sitting next to you, you may well be convinced that what you "saw" is the correct and that what the other fellow "saw" is incorrect. Of course, the other fellow comes away with the opposite conclusion.

As an example of selective perception, in the Fall of 2009 I read a newspaper article about the appearance of a politician on a popular television show. The journalist who wrote the article was not impressed with the interview, feeling that the politician's answers to a number of questions were hesitant and inconsistent. A few days later, I saw another article in a different paper which reported that the interview went quite well; that the politician was confident and gave very professional responses to the questions.

When two people develop diametrically opposite responses to the same event one has to wonder if the "Relativists" are right. Is there really an objective reality? Do we need another Dr. Johnson kicking a stone to refute Berkeley? Majoo's explanation of such discrepancies seems useful. The bias caused by the filtering of the vast amount of information available to us today clearly affects thinking processes.

So instead of asking how much someone knows, perhaps we should ask if they have inquiring minds (*cf.* Peirce). Do they ask questions? Going back a step, do they know enough about a subject to ask questions, and are they confident enough to ask them? Can teachers provide students with a background that will make them inquisitive? What sort of background would that be?

When I read articles on improving the scientific literacy of the average person they focus on the need to evaluate decisions about government funding of scientific projects. The topics mentioned tend to be things such as global warming, stem cell research, large particle accelerators, etc. But decisions about these topics are not made by members of the general population on their scientific merits: they are made by politicians, who, regardless of their understanding of science, usually base their decisions on political and economic criteria. So, the large-scale topics are not relevant; in fact, decisions that strongly affect the average person pertain mainly to local matters.

For example, someone who is appointed to a local plan commission or zoning board occasionally has to make decisions about technical matters. Will development of some tract of land change its drainage properties to the extent that neighboring areas will be flooded? Should the county install a sewer system in an older subdivision in which septic systems are malfunctioning? Should the city annex an adjacent area to prevent development over the recharge zone for its water wells? When people propose or protest projects of these types they often bring engineers with them to discuss the technical merits or pitfalls. Which set of experts should be believed? Is it likely that anyone on the board will know enough to ask relevant questions? How does the average person, appointed to such a board make decisions about these matters?

How do we get average people to be sufficiently inquisitive to learn enough about technical matters that they can function effectively on such boards, or that they can ask relevant questions of board members at their meetings? The educational system cannot anticipate all of the possible situations the average person will face, so questions about what sort of scientific background people should have are not easy to answer.

The standard (and inadequate) answer to such questions involves providing students with a broad-based liberal arts education, because such programs usually require one or two one-semester courses in science. Can that approach do the job? The answer is no, it cannot. Such courses tend to be introductory survey courses that cover too many topics to be able to go into any of them in much detail. Students come away with a smattering of knowledge, which to be effective, would have to be reinforced in subsequent years to become permanent parts of their mental equipment (Schank's concept of overlaying material on what is already stored in one's memory is relevant here).

> Recall the woman who indicated that all she remembered about one of my courses was that I spoke English correctly. No overlaying there.

Where can the necessary reinforcement come from? Not from television. It is not clear how watching programs in the Discovery Channel will provide the needed reinforcement, because television programming rarely provides sequels, so what one learns watching a show today is not reinforced by whatever is covered the next week. In addition, television is a passive medium that does not require intellectual engagement. It is a perfect example of the "communications medium" model of learning, in which one assumes that something is learned because it has been transmitted and received. But in fact, little is learned unless something is done with what is received. Recall Francis Crick's comments on how the brain functions.

Perhaps the solution is to concentrate less on what people learn in school and to think about the people who do not stop learning when they finish school. Some people engage in activities throughout their lives that result in reasonably detailed knowledge of technical information. For example, many famers know as much about the local soils and drainage as the average civil engineer. And well drillers can be a resource on water supplies. These people did not learn what they know to satisfy a degree requirement imposed by an academic committee. Their knowledge represents an excellent example of "situated" learning because they learned about things in context. Many of them are intellectually active people who are less likely to be intimidated by experts, so many local communities may have more people who can provide guidance on technical matters than is realized. I wonder how often such people are appointed to oversight boards.

So perhaps the broad definition of scientific literacy is not a cop-out. Perhaps our emphasis on formal educational programs has been biasing estimates of scientific literacy of the general population.

McDermott noted that much of the traditional approach to science education uses deductive logic that introduces a general principle and then applies it to a few special cases. We expect students to be able to understand this approach regardless of the fact that it might have taken the instructor years to develop a conceptual model of the discipline, and perhaps hours to construct a particular lecture. Yet students are expected to understand the material merely because it is presented clearly and coherently. Worse, they are expected to infer and assimilate the conceptual model underlying the subject in a few minutes.

If it were possible for students to internalize abstract material while hearing someone talk about it, they would quickly know enough to be able to advance the subject. By "standing on the shoulders" of the instructor, the students would be able to make major breakthroughs fairly quickly. Taking this idea a bit further, after a generation or two perhaps we could expect senior theses to approach Nobel Prize quality.

But we do not see the kinds of results this approach should produce. We do not see large numbers of scientifically literate students graduating each year. It is clear that the logic behind the traditional way science is taught is flawed. Yet we persist.

Is science part of, or can it be made part of the average person's life? A comparison with sports suggests that the answer is negative. The television news announcer can assume his audience knows the details of sports such as basketball and football because everyone grows up knowing about sports. In the public schools everyone took "gym" classes every year, and because of the nature of these classes, everyone participated.

Those last two points are important enough to repeat: *everyone* took gym classes, and *everyone* participated. At different grade levels we participated in activities such as gymnastics, softball and basketball. Outside of school, we saw these sports on television, and live, when "our team" played teams from other schools. Some of us also played sandlot baseball, football or basketball. Even those who do not now participate in sporting events have not abandoned thinking about them. Communities participate vicariously as their schools' teams compete. The attention and acclamation given to the team members reinforces them psychologically, and convinces them and everyone else in the community that their efforts are worthwhile. It may even be accurate to say that anyone who is not "sports literate" is not participating in American culture.

Nothing like this psychological support is available for activities that are not related to sports. Even the school bands exist primarily to play at sporting events. There certainly is no community infrastructure to support science in the schools comparable to what is behind sports programs. The science fairs that are held each year are not nearly comparable in interest to the weekly high school basketball games, because the community is not involved in the science fairs. The clerk at the hardware store is much more likely to know how many points you scored in a game last month than how well your project was rated at the local science fair last week. We can improve the education of teachers, develop better teaching materials, and spend more money on the physical facilities of the schools, but we cannot expect to develop a level of scientific literacy in the general public that is in any way comparable to the general level of sports literacy.

The marked difference in value afforded sports and science in America is ironic because few people would claim that sports provide benefits to society comparable to those provided by science and technology. Sports may provide a sense of accomplishment to the players, but regardless of what coaches say about the importance of teamwork and sacrifice, the skills associated with sports activities do not prepare anyone for a career as a scientist or engineer or accountant or stock broker or journalist, etc. The next generation does not benefit from the actions of today's athletes, yet our society holds many more athletes up as role models than scientists. And the few scientists whose names people recognize may be known for non-scientific activities (e.g. Richard Feynman played the bongo drums).

Perhaps this paradox can be explained by noting that because most people had experiences with sports in school they do not feel that the activities of college and professional athletes are too far beyond their own abilities. Of course they usually are wrong about that, but at the very least, the average person feels qualified to evaluate the performance of a player or team. On the other hand, because few people in society "participated" in science, they have no idea what scientists do. A discussion in a barbershop may well center on how well a pitcher does against the Red Sox, but one doubts that the conversation often is about Buckeyballs or the merits of funding the Superconducting Supercollider project.

So we should not wonder why students do not respond to the subjects of our lectures in introductory service courses with enthusiasm. Science is not an important part of their lives.

In the interest of full disclosure, I will admit that I lost all interest in sports when the Dodgers left Brooklyn.

In "...present-day America, theories of language teaching are more articulate and better organized than is the culturally patterned ability to learn a foreign language."
Margaret Mead

We cannot even say *that* much about science education and the learning of science in America because the way we teach science courses is not based on any principles. Those who teach most of the science courses in colleges today are scientists who have no background in educational psychology, so most just teach the way they were taught. The result is that we want to change American culture by making everyone more scientifically literate but we think that the change can be accomplished by telling people that it is important for them to learn more about science, and we do it in courses that are not effective learning venues.

Of course, we can say the same things about the teaching of History or Literature. Facts can be conveyed but not motives.

> "When it is available, scientific knowledge is more reliable, on the whole than non-scientific...In a discipline where there is a scientific consensus the amount of certain knowledge may be limited, but it will be honestly labeled: 'Trust your neck to this,' or 'this ladder was built by a famous scholar, but no one else has been able to climb it.'"
> **John Ziman**

How many people actually believe such statements? When the public is involved in decision-making the results are erratic. Consider the controversy over fluoridation of drinking water. Blume noted that between November, 1950 and December, 1966, there were 952 referenda on the subject. In 566 cases (59%) fluoridation was rejected. The public *was told* about the health benefits of fluoridation, but clearly, a substantial number of people rejected *what was told them*.

The key seems to be the word "told." Due to the nature of the topic (biochemistry), few of those who voted against fluoridation could have understood the details, so it also seems reasonable to say that few who voted *for* fluoridation could have understood them either. The results of the referenda probably were due to how many people had confidence in the scientific groups that were advocating the project.

If you do not understand the details of a scientific project, it is no more rational to *accept* what the authorities say than to *reject* what they say. To accept authoritative statements is to assume that scientists are objective, disinterested, and knowledgeable. To reject the statements involves not making those assumptions. To make or to reject such assumptions frees people from the work involved in learning about the topic.

One wonders if a better understanding of science could have changed attitudes about fluoridation. The scientific literacy of the public should be better today than 50 years ago. But the alienation caused by fear of large-scale public health projects and fear of experiments with drugs persists. Today there is a controversy over whether vaccinations are the cause of autism in children. Those who wish to believe there is a causal relationship between the two are not convinced by studies showing no relationship.

And why should they? Few people know enough about statistics to be comfortable with a study when they are told that the results are "statistically significant."

And according to surveys, the consensus among climate scientists that human activities are causing global warming has been discounted by more than half of the population. People do not want to accept the conclusion that large societal changes are necessary to prevent global warming, so they reject the statements by the experts that warming is occurring.

When scientists use the "argument from authority," they set themselves up for a fall. It is foolish to expect the public to accept what you say merely because you are a scientist. Many people see no reason to buy into what they consider to be your "belief system." They have their own, and are not willing to abandon it merely because you have several college degrees. They do not understand that science is not a belief system in the sense that *laissez faire* economics is one.

Science is an empirically-based search for understanding. Scientific results are tentative, in that they will be discarded if shown to be incorrect by future studies. But most people feel that their beliefs are True and feel threatened by attempts to imply that their beliefs may be wrong.

It is certainly true that the public is more aware of science today than it was 50 years ago, but it is not at all clear that people have a better understanding of it.

How does a standard liberal arts education prepare students to deal with the world? Those who go through such a program specialize in some subject (e.g. Economics, Sociology, English, History, etc.) and "dip into" other areas. The standard core curriculum requires one or two courses in composition, history, social sciences, mathematics and science. With the exception of composition, in which students spend much of their time writing and being graded on their writing, this kind of program does not usually require much in the nature of "hands-on" experiences. Writing a term paper for a history course provides more detailed information about a period than is covered in the lecture component of the course, but it does not prepare a student to do what historians do with information - that is, fit what they get from their sources into a framework that explains something about the period. Explanation, not exposition is what historians do. And writing a paper in an economics course does not prepare one to read the economics literature (an advanced degree in mathematics may be needed for that). So perhaps my criticism of the introductory survey courses in science is not fair. The courses provide a once-over-lightly view of a discipline (as do the survey courses in the social sciences), and that is all they were intended to do.

One problem with the introductory survey courses that is not discussed very often is that much of the time they are the only science courses taken by elementary school teachers. Experience tells me that few of these teachers remember much about the subject once the course has been completed, so their ability to get kids excited about science is questionable.

For example, my sister's roommate in college took one geology course. When she was student teaching in an elementary school a kid handed the woman a rock to identify. She looked at it and said that it was a piece of granite. Then the kid said "my father is a geologist and he says it's a limestone." Once she got over the desire to strangle the kid she must have wondered how much credibility she had after that experience.

To be fair, identifying a small rock specimen is not easy, especially if it was found in a stream bed and has been smoothed over by tumbling in the current. But if anyone should have more than a smattering of knowledge of science, it should be those who teach kids when they are still curious about things. Unfortunately, we do not usually require that elementary teachers take any more than the absolute minimum number of science courses in order to graduate.

I am not one of those who believe that substituting knowledge of content for knowledge of educational psychology is the key to improving teacher education programs; most of the people who make that argument have never tried to teach; their recommendations are proof of the adage that every complex problem has a simple solution - one that is wrong. But it is also true that with the exception of exceptionally charismatic teachers, one cannot interact effectively with kids who are curious about scientific subjects without some background in science.

This is not to say that knowledge of content is not important. I read an article once about teaching mathematics in which an instructor felt that a course in Number Theory was invaluable to her because she understood why things work out the way they do. She would not quote theorems in Number Theory to respond to students' questions, but because she understood the foundations she could understand why students' might believe some things about numbers, and she could formulate meaningful responses to questions.

But many content experts are not as perceptive as that instructor. There is a story about the diva, Maria Callas, who tried to give master classes when she retired from singing. The classes were a disaster because she had never "thought about" singing, she just did it. She could not explain how students could improve, she could just try to show them how to sing. And this was after her voice was "gone," so she could not even do that well.

In a discussion of what is involved in learning to read, Gilbert Ryle suggested that we do not usually consider the effort successful until children can read things they have not yet been exposed to. If we apply that criterion to scientific literacy, should we require that a person be capable of saying sensible things about new material? The men who administered the oral examinations I took in graduate school thought so. Is that too restrictive at lower educational levels?

In order to understand one discipline reasonably well, you have to know some things about other disciplines. The Biologist must be comfortable with Chemistry; the Physicist must be fluent in Mathematics; etc. Undergraduate science programs respond to that criterion but it is not clear how successful any other type of program can be in enhancing scientific literacy if it does not provide broad exposure to the sciences.

"We require students to take science in school, but we teach the courses in such a way that few students can develop any understanding of the material. Then we complain that the public is scientifically illiterate."
de Caprariis (1997)

The temptation to quote myself was irresistible. The quotation comes from a paper I wrote that attempts to examine introductory science courses the way an Anthropologist might examine a culture. It makes use of a device described by Gregory Bateson, which involved what he called the digital code of written text. He noted that if a message written in English is represented by

(first part / second part)

and the slash mark divides a word at the letter "t," we can say that the next letter will mostly likely be an "h," an "r," or a vowel. Note that one must be reasonably fluent in English to "cross the slash mark" in this way. Those who do crossword puzzles are assisted by such rules. The rules are culturally constructed.

Bateson was more interested in the meaning of the code than that of the message. He defined "meaning" as pattern, redundancy, or information. He did this because an art object (which is iconic rather than digital) is internally patterned, and at the same time is part of a cultural pattern.

[Characteristics of an object / Characteristics of its culture]

As an Anthropologist, Bateson wondered what sort of rules enable us to move from left to right, across this statement. It seems clear that we must understand those rules to understand why the message conveyed by an object is relevant to a culture. For example, although we admire the pictures painted on the walls of caves in Altimira and Lasceaux, we have no idea what messages they were intended to convey because we know nothing about the Pleistocene culture in which they were created. One must know the rules in order to move across the slash marks in statements about a culture.

Wittgenstein doubted that we can ever completely understand the rules of some other culture, and with respect to the cave paintings, he might have been correct. We have no idea what message the painter of a bison on a cave wall intended to send because the picture alone cannot illustrate the rules of the culture. To illustrate this point, consider the difference between a mime and a dancer. The mime suggests everyday activities.

[mime representing climbing a ladder / climbing a ladder]

The code is clear because the mime does things we know how to do. He exaggerates movement, but we see him doing routine things. He shows us what we normally do, so we have little difficulty crossing the slash mark. On the other hand, consider

[dancer portraying the death of a swan / death of a swan]

Here the representation is not only iconic, but the dancer is conveying thoughts and emotions as well as activities. To cross the slash mark the audience must fill in more here than it must in the case of the mime's performance.

Even if I practice the moves used by a dancer, I will not necessarily be able to cross the slash mark. The ability to mimic the moves has nothing to do with comprehending the emotions intended by the moves. If I become familiar with the things dancers do I may be able to say, at some point, that the next move will likely be a knee bend, but just because I understand the mechanics (the grammar) of the dance does not mean I will understand the iconic representations.

Now take it a step further.

[(dancer portraying the death of a swan / death of a swan) / Western culture]

You must be able to cross the first slash mark to be able to cross the second one. That is, first you must understand abstract representations, and then you must understand how an abstract representation of an activity can be embedded in a story that is meaningful to the culture. Which story is not important: that a story is told in this manner is what is important.

Now consider the statement:

[Research experience in a laboratory / Science as done by practitioners]

As in the example of the mime, the internal patterns on either side of the slash mark are similar, if not identical. But this statement is not what students encounter in science courses in school. There they are faced with

[Statements made about doing science / Science as done by practitioners]

The internal patterns on the left side of the slash mark are due mainly to the topic that is discussed orally, whereas the internal patters on the right side of the slash mark are due mainly to the choices made about what to study.

The difference between the two sets of internal patterns is due to the fact that we rarely do things as systematically as we explain the subject after the work is done.

Francis Crick (1988), writing about of the steps involved in determining the structure of the DNA molecule, noted that scientific research is performed by human beings, not by the "...stereotyped emotionless scientist solving problems by rigid logic."

Although the explanations given in a classroom provide factual information, rarely do they convey the sense of actually doing science. As in the case of the person learning the moves made by a dancer, students cannot internalize what it means to do science by listening to someone talk about science.

The rules are not obvious to the students in the class. They listen and take notes about what they are told, but they cannot possibly understand how or why the work was done. Even if we *tell* them how and why the work was done, rarely will they realize that that information is at a higher level (involving meta-statements) than the factual information presented. They will just write it in their notebooks, as something to be memorized for a test.

An Anthropologist once said that if you wish to learn about a culture, don't watch what the people do; look at what they take for granted. It would appear that we take for granted that the elementary school teachers charged with educating our children and grandchildren need have no more understanding of basic science courses than what they may remember years after taking one or two introductory survey courses in science. A code indicates something about a culture. Paraphrasing William James, like it or not, the way we teach science conveys ontological information about our culture.

Charles Curtis wrote about an actress who claimed that

> "...she could portray any emotion from the wings,
> showing only one foot and her elbow."

He went on to say that the more traditions and assumptions she and her audiences shared, the more she could imply "from the wings." and that their common understanding was largely implicit. The members of the audience could "cross the slash marks" because they knew the rules.

> "(A culture is) a way of living and to be understood, it
> must be seen as offering a set of resources for speech
> and conduct...and a set of things that it is possible to
> do..."
> **James Boyd White**

We can assume that the artists who crawled a mile into caves in France and Spain, using torches for light, to paint images of cattle, bison and men on the walls did so for a purpose, even if we can never discover the purpose because we have no idea of the rules that provided the foundation for their society.

> To paraphrase Wittgenstein, if you do not know the rules you cannot understand the culture. And he felt that we hardly ever understand other peoples' rules.

The activities going on at a university are easy to observe. People go to classes, take notes, study for tests, socialize in the snack bar, look up things in the library, etc. A stranger to our culture could mimic these activities without ever understanding the reasons they are being done. Some students (many?) do not accomplish much more than that. They mimic what others do and they learn some of the rules of the system. They learn how the physical system is organized but they do not really understand the set of rules.

In a university it is possible to get a degree by doing many of the activities but not understanding much of what is behind them. That is partly the fault of the system. After all, we are not trying to produce large numbers of scholars, so the majority of students never really penetrate very deeply into academic culture.

Of course they do penetrate the culture associated with fraternities and sororities, but that is because what is learned there is "situated."

Consider our educational system in terms of the medieval apprentice system. The apprentice started out by doing mundane things, such as sweeping the floor and stoking the fire. Over a period of time the activities assigned to him reflected more of those done by the master. The apprentice practiced a task until he mastered it. Contrast that with the experience of a typical college student who does a task once or twice, is tested on it, and then may never see it again. A vague recollection may remain in the minds of students but certainly not competence.

The most important part of the academic culture consists of categorizing information. Using the information is for the scholars - the specialists - but understanding the nature and utility of categorization would benefit every student, because it is a "meta" skill.

Cognition involves thinking about something - geology, physics, history, economics, etc. Thinking about how one thinks about those topics is called meta-cognition. The categories into which knowledge is divided involve meta-cognition. They are constructed for a purpose: that of understanding the material efficiently.

Most introductory courses involve cognition because they are concerned with a transfer of information (not necessarily an understanding of it). Many definitions have to be learned before one can do much in a discipline. A new vocabulary is involved in most cases. Even at this level, some meta-cognition comes into play, in that the course is broken down into categories. For example, an introductory Oceanography course typically has three sections:

the Geology of the Ocean Basins, the Properties of Ocean Water, and Life in the Oceans. These categories represent convenient ways to think about the subject covered in the course; they allow students to concentrate their efforts on one aspect of a complex topic at a time. Each of these categories is then subdivided, as the instructor covers the details of each one. The rationale underlying the breakdown into categories and sub-categories is not usually discussed in these courses, partly because the curriculum is already crammed with topics, and partly because most students would not understand the relevance of such a discussion. Many would just ask if this "stuff" would be on the next test.

It seems reasonable to say that a definition of scientific literacy (perhaps it should be called "scholarly" literacy because it is relevant to non-science disciplines too) would include the understanding of meta-cognitive processes. It would help their progress greatly if students understood that the categories used to define aspects of a subject are useful constructs rather than natural laws. They impose order on natural phenomena in a way that facilitates the overlaying process needed to produce Schank's semantic memories.

"The scientist tries to account for what he sees...Did anyone discover the proton? No, he just found a need for such a notion in order to talk about what he could observe."
Wendell Johnson

"There is no definitive history of anything; there are
only histories, human interventions which do not give
us the answer, but give us only those answers called
forth by the questions that have been asked."
Neil Postman (1993)

Scientists construct concepts according to what they see, and
when the concept does not fit the observations it is discarded and
a new one constructed. That is appropriate because the concept
is man-made. Historians do the same thing. Unfortunately, most
people continue to view the world using old concepts because
they do not understand that their beliefs are man-made.

"...rationality isn't an endowment but an achievement
that can come undone at any moment. And that is just
why it is prudent, in my opinion to distrust sacrosanct
authorities, whether academic or psychiatric or
ecclesiastic, and to put one's faith instead in objective
procedures that can place a check on our never-sated
appetite for self-deception."
Frederic Crews

This is good advice (even though it got Galileo into trouble), and
it pertains to any field of endeavor. The words "rationality is an
achievement" should be posted at the entrance to every school. But
even those who recognize is as a hard-won achievement sometimes
succumb to temptation, as indicated by the next comment.

"There is one great difficulty with a good hypothesis.
When it is completed and rounded, the corners smooth
and the content cohesive, it is likely to become a thing
in itself, a work of art. It is then like a finished sonnet
or a painting completed. One hates to disturb it. Even

if subsequent information should shoot a hole in it, one
hates to tear it down because it once was beautiful and
whole."
John Steinbeck.

Scientists are human, so sometimes it is tempting to avoid
admitting that one's hypothesis is not correct. The book from
which this quotation came was largely written by Steinbeck, but
this statement was probably due to his friend, Ed Ricketts, a marine
Biologist (and the model for the main character in Steinbeck's
novel *Cannery Row*), who was on the voyage Steinbeck wrote
about. A person can learn a lot about science by reading that
book.

"The prevailing preoccupation with the psychic,
the mystic and the occult makes it apparent that an
alarming number of adults cannot tell sense from
nonsense."
Fred Hechinger

The statement is taken from a national Research Council panel
report that Hechinger used in an article on science education. It
makes one wonder what the emphasis on science education after
the Soviet Union launched Sputnik in 1957 has accomplished. It
seems clear that attempts to make science understandable to the
public has had mixed results. Those who believe in the occult
include many people who have had one or more science courses.

Bertrand Russell was a philosopher who sometimes wrote about
science. In one of his collections of essays he noted that it is not
important *what* opinions are held as long as they are held

"...tentatively, and with a consciousness that
new evidence may at any moment lead to their
abandonment. This is the way in which opinions are
held in science, as opposed to the way in which they
are held in theology. The decisions of the Council of
Nicaea are still authoritative, but in science fourth-
century opinions no longer carry any weight."

This approach to knowledge is similar to that in the quotation by
Peirce found at the beginning of this chapter. In the same essay,
Russell (1950) said:

"Scientific theories are accepted as useful hypotheses to
suggest further research, and as having some element
of truth in virtue of which they are able to colligate
existing observations; but no sensible person regards
them as immutably perfect."

To the extent that they have "some element of truth," hypotheses
provide a framework that can be used to think about phenomena.
This is also consistent with Peirce's statement. Hypotheses also
provide a target, because scientists who are not convinced that a
particular hypothesis provides an adequate explanation try to find
counterexamples which can be used to topple the thing from its
pedestal. This is a healthy approach if learning about the world is
your goal.

Most people do not realize that science is a competitive business.
For example, if you submit a paper to a professional journal
claiming that tests you conducted show that process A could not
produce result B, the editors will send the manuscript to two or
three scientists who are experts in either A or B or both to get
their opinions about your claim. The reviewers will examine the
design of your experiment and the manner in which you analyzed

the data. If they cannot find any flaws in your work, the paper will probably be published. Then the controversy begins. Quite often, those who believe that A *does in fact* cause B may try to duplicate your tests to see if they get the same results. The important thing is that they will not just deny your claims; instead, they will go out of their way to show that you are wrong *by doing work themselves*. If their results contradict yours, their work will go through the same review process before being published, and you may be one of the reviewers.

So there are two levels of review for most scientific claims: the formal reviewing process by the journal and the informal review by readers of the journal who may attempt to duplicate your results to see if they are correct. Merely stating that someone is wrong is not sufficient: to be believed, you must *show* that the other fellow is wrong. The peer review process described here is not perfect: sometimes things get published that are wrong, because either the reviewers were not as careful as they might have been or because the tests used to get results were not described completely enough for the reviewers to notice problems. The controversy over "cold fusion" is an example. Two respected scientists claimed (at a news conference, not in a paper submitted to a journal), that they caused the nuclei of atoms to fuse together at room temperature and pressure, resulting in the release of a large amount of energy. If true, the process they described could produce large amounts of inexpensive energy for society. But no one else could duplicate their results. Eventually, other scientists showed that the data collected in the original experiments were misinterpreted. The point is that other scientists did not just write letters claiming that the results were wrong: they *showed* that the results were wrong.

A story about the physicist Wolfgang Pauli shows another aspect of how science is done, as opposed to how the results are described in textbooks. After a presentation at a conference, someone asked Pauli his opinion of the work the speaker described. He just shrugged and said that the results "were not even wrong."

Pauli was a tough audience but his point was that the speaker had studied a problem so simple that the results probably were correct. If he had been studying a challenging problem the results would have been wrong, but in determining why they were wrong, the profession would have learned why the problem was more subtle than everyone thought. Progress is not made by solving what can be solved easily. Topics that lead to a deeper understanding of how things work have many layers of complexity; they are the topics that one should spend one's time on. But how do we explain that to students in an introductory course? Or to the Congressional Committees which oversee the budgets at the National Science Foundation or the National Institutes of Health?

According to Primo Levi, someone once wrote to Aldous Huxley asking for advice on how to become a writer. Huxley advised the fellow to buy two cats, watch how they interact with each other and describe the interactions. That is not a trivial response because observing and describing how two cats interact would be good practice for learning to describe how people interact, which is what a novelist does. I mention this example because a systematic study of how two organisms interact is one kind of scientific study. Someone who can do what Huxley advised should be well on the way to satisfying Peirce's criterion of scientific literacy.

From time to time a Creationist suggests that a debate about Evolution would be appropriate, and volunteers to debate anyone and everyone on the subject. There is no point in accepting such a challenge because to do so would give credibility to positions that are not defensible. I suspect that no Biologist would be willing to enter into a debate about extra-terrestrial life with someone who claims to receive radio signals from aliens through the fillings in his teeth, and for the same reason, no one should be willing to debate a Creationist. In accepting such a challenge the scientist would be implicitly saying that the "other side's" position is respectable enough to discuss, and that sensible people should be willing to evaluate its validity. But anyone who believes that the material in the books of the Old Testament is literally true must also believe that the Earth is flat and is at the center of the Solar system. One cannot have a useful discussion with someone who really believes those things.

Another way to express this point is to say that there is no point in debating a subject which is not appropriate for a debate. An example of a topic that *is* appropriate for a debate is "Resolved: That the United States should withdraw from the United Nations." This is a topic that we can disagree about because we all have opinions about international affairs. Each of us could study the U.N. charter and decide whether we think the U.S. should belong to the organization. The winner of such a debate is usually the one who is more experienced in crafting arguments and speaking in public. On the other hand, if the example was "Resolved: That Evolution is the foundation of modern Biology," there would be nothing to debate, because the phrase is a statement of fact, not opinion. To reject the statement is to reject the last 150 years of biological science, which is not done lightly.

It is useful to note that with very few exceptions, those who do not believe in the theory of Evolution know little or nothing about Biology or Geology, so, although they usually deny it, the basis for their disagreement *has* to be religious in nature, not scientific. If you think about it, you never hear that an atheist claimed that the earth was created in six days about 6,000 years ago, or that the planet was covered by a universal flood once. Only fervent religious believers say such things, those who insist on a literal interpretation of the Bible. Most scientists recognize that the moral messages that are taught by the various religious denominations are what is important, not the manner in which the messages are constructed.

In short, a debate about evolution would be meaningless because the two sides of such a debate could not communicate. Recall Wittgenstein's comment about understanding a lion.

Unfortunately, the media contribute to the tendency to sponsor such debates by assuming that both sides of every controversy are of equal weight. Remember, if all conflicting opinions are of equal value, none of them can be "right." I believe it was Edward R. Murrow who pointed out the fallacy of believing that all opinions are of equal weight when he said that to the media, the comments of Judas and Jesus are of equal value.

It should not be necessary to point out that the basis of the last few paragraphs is not the "argument from authority," but many people will believe that. So consider the following:

> "The question, of course, is how an outsider can be sure that one school of thought is less entitled to our trust than a rival one...Certain instances of bad faith, however, are unmistakable: persistence in claims that have already been exploded; reliance on ill-designed studies, idolized law-givers, and self-serving anecdotes; evasion of objections and negative instances; indifference to rival theories and to the need for independent replication..."
> **Frederick Crews**

It is not easy to find a better set of criteria to use to evaluate conflicting claims about scientific matters. Bertrand Russell (1977) said some similar things, in his own, inimitable way.

> "I wish to propose for the reader's favourable consideration a doctrine which may, I fear, appear wildly paradoxical and subversive. The doctrine in question is this: that it is undesirable to believe a proposition when there is no ground whatever for supposing it to be true. I must, of course, admit that if such an opinion became common it would completely transform our social life and our political system; since both are at present faultless, this must weigh against it. In spite of ...(this), I maintain that a case can be made out for my paradox... "

> "The race does not always go to the swift
> Nor the fight to the strong.
> But that's the way to bet."
> **Grantland Rice**

This advice from a famous sports writer (adapted from *Ecclesiastes*) is a succinct way for the public to think about controversies involving topics such as Evolution and Global Warming. The consensus opinion is not always correct, but most people who bet on long shots lose their money.

If, for the last 50 years science teachers had been teaching how science is done, and if for the last 50 years students had been paying attention, one would not expect a substantial percentage of the population to decide that they can pick and choose from among the scientific results they will choose to accept.

The problem is that most science curricula *do not* stress how science is done; instead, they cover things scientists have discovered. Teachers can explain concepts such as genetics, gravity, electromagnetism, plate tectonics, etc., but cannot really teach students how the discoveries were made. I can tell a class that Newton did this, and Maxwell did that, and Watson and Crick did something else, but it is not possible in a classroom, or even in a laboratory session to immerse students in the atmosphere prevailing when the discoveries were made.

That is why I suggested earlier that perhaps it is necessary to major in science to be able to appreciate the discoveries made by professional scientists. If you have not internalized the processes involved in doing science, you will not appreciate the results to the extent that a scientist can.

That is not to say that all of the money spent developing science curricula in the years following the launching of Sputnik was wasted. More kinds of science courses are taught today than 50 years ago, and in many respects the courses are better than in the past. But it is asking too much to expect one or two introductory survey courses, in which students are merely told things, to provide any reasonable degree of scientific literacy.

It is important to try to define scientific literacy because the effort forces us to think about what is involved in being comfortable with scientific thinking. Unamuno wrote that he was sure he did not understand *Don Quixote* the way Cervantes intended because he was not Cervantes. But he used what he learned from Cervantes to comment on European culture in the early 20th Century. In the same way, each of us who is thinking about science will come away from the effort with slightly different results because we are all different. But the more that we think about what is involved in doing science, the more overlap should exist between our understandings of the subject. And the more that members of the general population think about science, the more overlap should exist between their understandings and those of scientists.

EPILOGUE

The development of an educational system that stresses learning, that makes effective use of technology, and that results in a major improvement in the scientific literacy of the general population is left as an exercise for the reader.

REFERENCES

Adams, Douglas, 2005, *The Salmon of Doubt: Hitchhiking the Galaxy One Last Time*: New York, Ballantine Books.

Adams, Henry, 1928, *The Education of Henry Adams*: New York, the Book of America.

Agar, Michael, 1994, *Language Shock: Understanding the Culture of Conversation*: New York, William Morrow and Company.

Auden, W. H., 1970, *A Certain World: A Commonplace Book*: New York, The Viking Press.

Bateson, Gregory, 1972, *Steps to an Ecology of Mind*: New York, Ballantine Books.

Blume, Stuart, 1974, *Toward a Political Sociology of Science*: New York, The Free Press.

Butterfield, Herbert, 1965, *The Whig Interpretation of History*: New York, W. W. Norton & Co.

Calvino, Italo, 1972, *Invisible Cities*: New York, Harcourt Brace Javanovich, Publishers.

Chesterton, G. K., 1904, *The Napoleon of Notting Hill*: London, John Lane, The Bodley Head.

-------------- 1927, *The Return of Don Quixote*: London, Chatto & Windus.

Crews, Frederick, 2006, *Follies of the Wise: Dissenting Essays*: Emeryville, CA, Shoemaker and   Hoard.

Crick, Francis, 1988, *What Mad Pursuit*: New York, Basic Books.

--------------, 1994, *The Astonishing Hypothesis*: New York, Simon & Schuster.

Curtis, Charles, 1957, *A Commonplace Book*: New York, Simon and Schuster.

de Caprariis, Pascal, 1997, Impediments to Providing Scientific Literacy to Students in Introductory Survey Courses: *Journal of Geoscience Education*, vol. 45, p. 107-210.

Deming, W. Edwards, 1986, *Out of the Crisis*: Cambridge, M.I.T. Center for Advanced Engineering Study.

Dyson, Freeman, 1997, *Imagined Worlds*: Cambridge, Harvard University Press.

Gay, J. and M. Cole, 1967, *The New Mathematics and An Old Culture*: New York, Holt, Rinehart, & Winston.

Geertz, Clifford, 1973, Thick Description: Toward an Interpretive theory of Culture, p. 3-30, in *The Interpretation of Cultures*: New York, Basic Books.

Getman, Julius, 1992, *In the Company of Scholars*: Austin, University of Texas Press.

Gladwin, Thomas, 1970, *East is a Big Bird*: Cambridge, Harvard University Press.

Hazlitt, William, 1949, On going on a Journey: in *The Essays of William Hazlitt*: London, Macdonald & Co. (First published in 1822.)

Hechinger, Fred, 1980, (Editorial column on science education): *New York Times*, January 29, 1980.

Illich, Ivan, 1972, *Deschooling Society*, New York, Harper & Row.

James, William, 1929, *The Varieties of Religious Experience: A Study in Human Nature*: New York, The Modern Library.

Johnson, Wendell, 1972, *Living with Change*: New York, Harper and Row.

Klinkenborg, Verlyn, 2007, Wiring the Frog, or Personal Tales from the Electronic Present, *New York Times*, August 16, 2007, p. A24

Lanham, Richard, 1993, *The Electronic Word: Democracy, Technology and the Arts*: Chicago, University of Chicago Press.

Le Guin, Ursula, 1989, *Dancing at the Edge of the World: Thoughts on Words, Women, Places*: NewYork, Grove Press.

-------------- 2004, *The Wave in the Mind: Talks and Essays on the Writer, the Reader, and the Imagination*: Boston, Shambala Publications.

Levi, Primo, 1989, *Other People's Trades*: New York, Summit Books.

Lord, Audre, 1984, *Sister Outsider: Essays and Speeches*: New York, The Crossing Press.

Majoo, Fahrad, 2008, *True Enough: Learning to Live in a Post-Fact Society*: New York, Wiley.

McCloskey, Donald, 1990, *If You're So Smart: The Narrative of Economic Expertise*: Chicago, University of Chicago Press.

McCorduck, Pamela, 1985, *The Universal Machine: Confessions of a Technological Optimist*: New York, Harcourt Brace Jovanovich, Publishers.

McDermott, L.C., 1993, Guest Comment: How we teach and how students learn - a mismatch?, in *American Journal of Physics*, vol. 61, no. 4, p. 295-298.

Mead, Margaret, 1964, *Continuities in Cultural Evolution*: New Haven, Yale University Press.

Moerman, Michael, 1988, *Talking Culture: Ethnography and Conversations Analysis*: Philadelphia, University of Pennsylvania Press.

Murray, Janet, 1997, *Hamlet on the Holodeck: the future of narrative in cyberspace*: New York, The Free Press.

O'Donnell, James, 1998, *Avatars of the Word*: Cambridge, Harvard University Press.

Ortega y Gasset, Jose, 1961, *Meditations on Quixote,* trans. by Evelyn Rugg and Diego Marin: New York, W.W. Norton & Co.

Peirce, Charles, 1955, *Philosophical Writings of Peirce*: ed. J. Buchler: New York, Dover Publications.

Postman, Neil, 1976, *Crazy Talk, Stupid Talk*: New York, Dell Publishing Co.

----------, 1988, *Conscientious Objections*: New York, Alfred Knopf, Inc.

----------, 1993, *Technolopy: The Surrender of Culture to Technology*: New York, Vintage Books.

----------, 1999, *Building a Bridge to the 18th Century: How the Past Can Improve Our Future*: New York, Vintage Books.

Richardson, V., 1990, Significant and Worthwhile Change in Teaching Practice: *Educational Researcher,* vol. no.19, no. 7, p. 10-18.

Rivoli, Pietra, 2005, *The Travels of a T-Shirt in the Global Economy*: New York, Wiley.

Russell, Bertrand, 1950, *Unpopular Essays*: New York, Simon and Schuster.

--------, 1977, *Skeptical Essays*: London, Unwin Paperbacks. First published in 1928.

Ryle, Gilbert, 1971, *Collected Papers*: vol. 2, New York, Barnes & Noble, Inc.

Schank, Roger, 1990, *Tell Me a Story: A New Look at Real and Artificial Memory*: New York, Charles Scribners Sons.

Steinbeck, John, 1971, *The Log from the Sea of Cortez*: New York, Bantam Books.

Unamuno y Hugo, Miguel, de, 1976, *Our Lord Don Quixote: The Life of Don Quixote and Sancho with Related Essays*: Princeton, Princeton University Press.

Valery, Paul, 1962, Orient and Occident, in *History and Politics*: Collected Works of Paul Valery, vol. 10, New York, Pantheon Books.

White James Boyd, 1984, *When Words Lose Their Meaning*: Chicago, University of Chicago Press.

Whitehead, Alfred North, 1929, *The Aims of Education*: New York, Mentor Books.

Wittgenstein, Ludwig, 1960, *Tractatus Logico-Philosophicus*: London, Routledge & Kegan Paul. (First published in 1922.)

--------- 1963, *Philosophical Investigations*: Oxford, Basil Blackwell.

Yekovich, F. and C. Walker, 1987, The Activation and Use of Scripted Knowledge; in Reading About Routine Activities: p. 145-176. in Britton, B., and S. Glynn (eds.), 1987, *Executive Control Processes in Reading*: Hillsdale, Laurence Erlbaum Assoc.

Ziman, John, 1968, *Public Knowledge, the Social Dimension of Science*: Cambridge, Cambridge University Press.

Zuboff, Shoshanna, 1988, *Work in the Age of the Smart Machine*: New York, Basic Books.

ABOUT THE AUTHOR

Pascal de Caprariis has spent most of his life trying to decide what to do when he grew up. Along the way, he progressed through the army, college, graduate school, working for a government contractor, more graduate school, teaching at a high school, and then at a university. All of those stages in his life prepared him for his current retirement activities that involve (with his wife) operating a yarn shop and a sheep farm.

He has enjoyed each of the stages of his life because they forced him to learn new things. And he revels in the fact that the current stage is forcing him to learn even more new things, mainly about running a business and about animal husbandry. A former city dweller, he and his wife now live on 20 acres along with 100 sheep, two alpacas, and several dogs and cats. Life is good.